Ashen Plains

Lilith A. Bennett

KITSAP
PUBLISHING

KITSAP PUBLISHING

Ashen Plains
First edition, published 2017

By Lilith Bennett
Cover design: Kitsap Publishing, iStock image license 16403258

ISBN-13: 978-1-942661-41-2

Published by Kitsap Publishing
P.O. Box 572
Poulsbo, WA 98370
www.KitsapPublishing.com

Printed in the United States of America

TD 20170104

50-10 9 8 7 6 5 4 3 2 1

Prologue

I'm dreaming again. It's the same dream I've been having off and on for the past two months. I'm alone on a train, bound for an unknown destination. My only company is a half empty bottle that smells of alcohol and the passing trees outside. It's strange since I don't even have a taste for such things. So what does it mean? What does any of this mean? Recently I trained myself to know when I'm dreaming. I did it hoping that it would allow me to figure out what's going on in this dream. Something about it bothers me. It's strange being so aware in a dream. You notice things here and there. Things that don't add up. Maybe a clock has a thirteen after the twelve, a person has two left hands and doesn't seem to realize it, or perhaps a familiar building is a different color than you remember. However, everything in this dream seems to remain consistent...and that's what bothers me.

I've never ridden a train in my life; never been near one. Pretty soon the dream is going to end the same way it always does, with me waking up screaming as my train ride comes to an abrupt end. I don't even know what to do anymore. I've tried everything I can think of. I've searched my pockets for clues, I've tried leaving the compartment and looking around, talking with the people I see. None of them ever say anything that makes sense. I tried telling my friend Annie about this dream after I started having it. Most of the time she's pretty good about making sense of them. In most cases there's some sort of hidden meaning to them. A warning, a message, something, anything.

I have my own theory about this dream. I'm an orphan living in an orphanage called Red Oak. I've been there ever since my aunt and uncle died. Been rather lucky, haven't I? First my parents die, I get passed off to my aunt and uncle, then they die, and now I'm stuck here in Red Oak; but I'll get to that later. My theory is that I'm afraid of what will happen if the orphanage closes down. I'm afraid that I'll be sent away. My parents died in a train accident when I was four. To be honest, I'm afraid to ride one.

That covers the train ride, the fact that I don't have a clue where it's heading, and the part where it goes off the rails. The last part being my fear of going the way of my parents, but why am I holding this bottle? That still stumps me. Maybe it's nothing. Just a piece of dream imagery that doesn't serve any real purpose. Most unusual of all is how my reflection is different from the one I see in my bedroom mirror every morning. I look older. In reality I'm sixteen, but this reflection appears to be around seven years older. Because of this one detail, I wondered for a brief time if perhaps this was a premonition of some sort. It didn't take me long to toss the idea aside. It seemed too far-fetched.

Outside, I can see a large windmill as the train passes by it. Every time the train passes it, I know the crash is about to occur. Any second now. I lean back and let out a sigh. This is the part where I wish I wasn't lucid. Even though I know it's coming, it's still terrifying. An explosion rattles the train and soon the compartment begins to quake. Before I can react, I'm hurled to the floor. I hear the sound of grinding and bending metal as the train leaves the tracks. There's a deafening crash and everything goes dark.

My eyes snap open and I'm back in my own bed, sweating and shaking. I suppose I can count myself lucky that I at least didn't scream this time. My roommate, Melissa always hates it when I wake her up like that. I can hear her snoring on the other side of the room. I would never hear the end of it if I woke her up even one more time. If I'm being completely honest, I can't stand her. She drives me up the wall. Red Oak has been facing some problems of its own in recent months. I'm not the only one who's afraid it might be closed down. It's something that the other wards have been talking about for a while now.

None of us want to leave, and Mr. Sullivan, the Headmaster is doing everything he can. I know he enjoys making a difference in our lives. Giving us a place to live, food to eat, shelter from the rain and wind. I worry for him as well. Doing the best I can to keep silent, I sneak out into the hall and close the door behind me. I wait for a moment and only leave when I'm certain I can still hear Melissa snoring. One of the things I love about this place is our library. It's not the largest I've seen, that much is true, but it's still wonderful nonetheless. That's where I'm heading now. I almost can't see in the darkened hallways. The hall lights are giving off a dim glow, but it's not much. Some of the bulbs have gone out in recent times and we haven't had the money to replace them. I suppose I should just be happy that we have any working ones at all.

At night most of the hall lights are switched off anyway. We can't afford to have them all running all the time. We do need at least a few on, though. Doesn't do us any good to have wards stumbling about in the darkness at night. I can just imagine the live-in medical staff losing it over a sudden stream of injured wards. It's bad enough that we have the occasional someone who falls on the stairs or becomes ill. Thankfully, such instances are rare. I've been one of the unfortunate few to tumble down the stairs. I ended up with a broken wrist. Not my idea of a good way to start the day.

As I reach the library door, I stop and glance down the hallway. I could have sworn I heard footsteps. With a quick shrug, I head through the door, being careful to close it without making a sound. It's so dark in here I almost can't see. A single sliver of moonlight is making its way in through a nearby window. There's just enough for me to see a lamp on a nearby table. As I go to switch it on, someone grabs my arm and pushes me down. I yelp as I hit the floor and immediately try to get back up. My attacker throws me back down and pins me. I struggle, but it's no use.

"Gotcha!" says a voice, "I'm getting fed up with you causing trouble around here." As soon as I hear her voice, I relax and let out a sigh.

"Sybil," I groan, "It's me."

"Wendy? What are you...? Hang on." Sybil lets go of me and turns on the nearby lamp. I squint as the light washes over me. She helps me to my feet and I brush myself off. A ghostly young woman stands before me. She looks as though she stepped out of a colorless photograph. That is, all except for her eyes. The irises of which are blood red. Her skin is deathly pale and her hair as dark as the night sky.

"Sorry about that," Sybil mumbles, stepping back and crossing her arms.

"What on earth do you think you're doing?" I snap, "Why would you attack me like that?"

"I said I was sorry," Sybil mutters, "What else do you want?"

"How about an explanation?"

"Of what?"

"Of why you're skulking about the library like a mugger on the prowl," I hiss.

"I thought you were someone else," Sybil explains. She uncrosses her arms and glances at the lamp. It's faint, but there's just enough light to see Sybil's black aura emanating from her arms, shoulders, and head. It's much like smoke from a fire. None of it reaches more than a few inches before it dissipates.

"On top of that, why are you wandering around this place at night?" she asks, plopping down in a rickety wooden chair.

"Since when do you care about that?" I mutter, sitting down across from her, "I couldn't sleep. I thought I'd come find a book."

"Seems a little unwise, don't you think?"

"It is if you're around..."

"I'm only kidding, Wendy," Sybil groans.

"Are you so bored in the Ashen Plains that you have to come here and cause trouble?"

"Yeah, sometimes," Sybil admits, "I have to say, I never thought being dead would be so dull." Glancing at Sybil's neck, I can see her hideous wound in the flickering light. She's been dead for about twenty years at this point. From what she's told me, she was decapitated in a factory accident when she was seventeen. They stitched her head back onto her body before she was buried.

"I suppose I can somewhat understand that," I yawn, "The Plains aren't the best place to spend eternity."

"It's better than the Black Abyss," Sybil shrugs.

"True..." I stare at a nearby bookshelf and begin to zone out. I'm thinking about that dream again. Why do I keep having it? What will it take to make it stop? Sybil's voice brings me back to reality and I rub my eyes.

"Something on your mind?" she asks.

"More than I would like," I sigh, "I don't even know where to begin."

"Well...start somewhere," Sybil smiles, "I've got all the time in the world."

Chapter 1

Sybil and I talked for over an hour before I felt like I could sleep again. I was surprised that no one interrupted us; considering the racket we must have caused during our little tussle. I told her about my dream, but she couldn't make heads or tails of it. I could tell she felt bad about that. She likes to be as helpful as possible and it seems to bother her when she doesn't have any advice to offer. In some ways, Sybil isn't the best person for me to discuss certain things with. While I was talking to her about the possibility of Red Oak closing down, I could tell she was worried for me, but not the way a living person would be. Sybil is a "Shadow", a spirit that dwells in one of the three Realms of the Dead. The Ashen Plains. The Plains are what some people might call "limbo," or "purgatory." It's not your best destination, but like she said the night before, it's far better than the Black Abyss.

The Abyss is what most would call "Hell" or the "underworld." It's a place of darkness, where souls wander the land, unable to feel anything other than hate, sorrow, and anger. The third is the Glowing Oasis. I imagine you already guessed it, but...yeah...it's what you would call "Heaven." I've never been to the Oasis or the Abyss, and I would be content to live out the rest of my days, and beyond that, without ever taking a trip to the latter. I've heard stories and that's enough for me.

The other realms have their own spirits. The ones who occupy the Oasis are called "Luminaries", and the ones who reside in the Abyss, are known as "Condemned." Of the three, Shadows have the most unique appearance. The Plains is the only world void of color. It's nothing but black, white, and shades of gray. Due to that, Shadows lack any color, save their eyes. Sybil has been dead long enough to have adapted to her situation. What I mean is that she doesn't remember things like illness, or hunger, or pain. Well, I'm sure she remembers...but she's at a point where it's hard for her to relate anymore. None of those things exist in the Plains. So when I tell her that I'm terrified that Red Oak might shut down, I don't think she understands how I feel.

I stare down at my plate, lost in thought as the noise of the dining hall drones on. Dozens of voices drown out the sound of my fork as I drag it along the plate. There's still plenty of food left, but I'm not hungry. Aside from my worries about Red Oak and my recurring dreams, I've had other things to worry about. Since I left my room this morning, I've been struggling to deal with a certain staff member standing nearby. She's had it out for me since I first came here. She doesn't like that I don't always listen to her.

Just this morning, she was hassling me about my "incessant daydreaming" as she put it. So what if I daydream while I'm here? It's not like I have much else to do. Living in an orphanage is far from every girl's dream. I decide to risk it and take a quick glance in her direction. Most of the time she finds someone else to bother by this point. It's already halfway through lunch. I can see that her back is turned, and all I can see is her long wavy, red hair. Her name is Miss Favela. At least that's what I call her. Right now she's talking to two other wards. No one I happen to know. I turn my attention back to my plate and continue to stare at it. I'd rather go back to my room. At least there I can escape this awful place. Even if it's only for a little while. I'm sure Sybil wouldn't object to me visiting her in the Plains. The girl beside me nudges me with her elbow.

"Wendy, are you alright?" the girl asks me. I glare at her for a moment and let out a groan.

"Has Miss Favela been giving you trouble again?"

"Of course she has," I mutter, "Why wouldn't she?"

"You should speak with Mister Sullivan about her," she continues, "I'm sure he'd be furious to know that one of his staff is mistreating his wards. It's not just you either; I've seen her bothering plenty of others."

"I don't want to bother him, Annie," I reply, "Mister Sullivan has done enough for me as it is. He has his hands full just trying to keep this place open."

"Oh, that's right," Annie sighs, "I've been trying to forget about that."

"Forget about what?"

"The fact that we may be homeless soon," she replies, setting her fork on her plate, "I don't know what I would do if that happened. Just the thought is enough to scare me."

"No need to worry," I assure her, "I'm certain Mister Sullivan will find some way to keep this place open. I imagine he'd be lost if Red Oak ever closed down. I don't want to be sent away anymore than you do, but I suppose we could end up somewhere better. Somewhere we don't have people like Miss Favela running amok."

"As much as I would enjoy that, I can't help but worry that we might end up somewhere worse."

"I know what you mean," I mumble.

"Have you heard what that bratty little wretch Melissa was doing this morning?" Annie asks me after swallowing a bite of potato.

"No," I grumble, "I don't care what that girl does anymore. It's always something terrible and often involves me."

"Is it sad that I find that to be true?" Annie asks.

"Welcome to my life, Annie."

"Anyway," she continues, clearing her throat, "I've heard that she was carrying on about something to do with you to the other wards."

"Like what?"

"Well, she claims you've been mumbling and shouting in your sleep for the past few nights. I hear she was repeating what she heard to everyone. Much to their amusement, of course. I swear, that girl is the devil."

"Trust me, I know someone who's worse than her," I grin, "If she wasn't my friend, that is."

"I find that hard to believe," she snorts.

"Her name is Sybil. I'll have to introduce the two of you sometime."

"Sybil?" she laughs, "There's no one here by that name. What are you talking about?"

"I didn't say she lived here," I reply, "I know her from somewhere else."

"And where would that be?" she asks, "Haven't you been here since you were nine?"

"Yep," I answer, "Seven years two weeks ago."

"So where did you meet her?"

"Somewhere close by, I'll say that much." I pick up my plate and head off to the kitchen. Annie does the same and follows after me.

"Somewhere close by?" she repeats, "Please Wendy, will you just tell me? I've had about enough of your vague answers."

"I'll explain later, Annie," I assure her, "Just...not right now. The last thing I need is someone overhearing me. I've already got plenty of others going on about how I'm not right in the head."

"Well, you are a bit strange," she admits, "Those bouts of daydreaming don't help." We place our plates and silverware on a counter and head back into the dining hall.

"I used to sit and read all the time," I continue, entering the dining hall, "but as it is, I've read everything that interests me. The library is only so big."

"Why don't you re-read the ones you like the most?" Annie suggests, "I do that sometimes."

"I've already tried that," I explain, "It's never the same. The first time you read a story, you don't know what's going to happen. The twists, the turns, they're all new to you. The problem is when you read it a second time it's not as exciting. It's boring. You know what will happen and when."

"I guess that's true," Annie admits, "Still, it's a nice distraction from what goes on around here. I guess I'm just not as picky as you."

"I suppose so..." We head through the dining hall and toward the courtyard. Just before we reach the doors, a hand grabs my shoulder. I turn to see Miss Favela glaring at me.

"Just where do you two think you're going?" she demands.

"Out to the courtyard ma'am," Annie explains, "We always go there after we eat."

"That's right, you do," Miss Favela replies, "but so does everyone else, and at the same time. Get back in the dining hall. Everyone will depart at the same time. That includes you troublemakers."

"Leaving a little early is hardly making trouble for anyone," I groan.

"I beg to differ, missy," Miss Favela snaps, leading us back to the dining hall, "Those two ornery Beckett brothers always find something they aren't supposed to do when the staff isn't around to watch them."

"That would be so awful if I were to sit and daydream now wouldn't it?" I reply, "Can't have any of that, now can we?"

"I've had just about enough of your sass Miss Warland," Miss Favela growls, "I've been putting up with it all week. Now go find a table and sit down." Annie rolls her eyes and we both head back to our table. Before we can get there, Melissa and her brother Albert show up.

"Wendy...Annie..." she smirks, "How are you?"

"Fine until you showed up," I mutter, "What do you want?"

"I wanted to tell you that we no longer have to share a room," she explains, "No more having to listen to your late night ramblings. Don't worry, if you ever wake up screaming again I'll be right down the hall."

"That's wonderful Melissa," I reply, "Now, would you care to repeat that without the attitude?"

"Seems I was mistaken," Melissa continues, "I thought you'd be happy."

"Oh, don't worry, I'm plenty happy," I mutter, "I just wish someone other than you had told me. That way I could insult you out of earshot. Just as you do with me."

"I'll be moving my things out tonight," Melissa informs me as she and Albert head toward the kitchen with their plates, "See you later."

"I think that's the first time she's ever said something I liked," Annie grumbles as we seat ourselves at a table.

"That may be so," I grunt, shifting my weight, "Although, I stand by what I said. It would've been nicer to hear it from someone else."

"Either way you get your own room," Annie grumbles, "If only we were all so lucky."

"Don't you have three people in your room?" I ask her.

"Yes," she nods, "Myself and two others."

"What if you were to take Melissa's place?" I suggest.

"That would be wonderful," she smiles, "No more having to live in a cramped room, and I would get to share a room with someone I like for once."

"We'll have to bring it up with Mister Sullivan later today," I reply, "I'm certain that he would at least consider it. He's a very reasonable man."

"So I've heard," Annie says, "I've asked him twice now for a room transfer. Seems that if others hadn't been thinking the same thing at the same time, I may have succeeded. Those two I live with drive me crazy."

"What do they do that's so terrible?" I ask.

"Several minor things that together frustrate me to no end," Annie groans, "They leave their things lying about and of course I end up tripping when I need to get up during the night. They both never shut up, I never get any peace and quiet unless they're either asleep or gone, they leave the window open for "fresh air" every night in spite of the weather, they're just...awful, both of them."

"Never would have guessed you felt that way," I reply, "They seem nice when I talk to them. What are their names again?"

"Maggie and Jasper," she answers, "And yes, they are nice...when you aren't forced to share a room with them. The worst part is that I never complain to either of them. I would feel guilty if I did."

"They're siblings, right?"

"Yes, they are," she replies, "They're inseparable...and sometimes insufferable..."

"Well, just hang on for at least one more night," I assure her, "I'm sure Mister Sullivan will think it a grand idea to have you stay with me."

"And what if he doesn't?"

"Good grief, Annie," I moan, "You're always so negative."

Chapter 2

Later that evening I find myself reluctantly assisting Melissa with gathering her possessions. As is the case with all wards, there isn't much to move. For once I can be thankful we have little. It means less time helping her.

"Is that everything?" I ask.

"I believe so," she replies, "I should go find someone to help me carry these down the hall. Lord knows you won't help me with them."

"Not with that attitude," I shoot back. She smirks and heads out of the room.

"Annoying little...ugh..." I growl, sitting down on the edge of my bed. I glance at the desk on the other side of the room. The clock on the wall says it's just past 7pm. I stand up and open one of the drawers. Inside I can see my black, leather-bound journal. I've had it for close to a year now. I'll admit, I didn't obtain it in the most honorable fashion. I stole it from a shop down the road. I've been afraid to go back ever since. I don't consider myself a thief, but I felt I had to have it. It gets lonely here, even with Annie and Sybil around; so I took to putting my thoughts on paper. As of now I don't have much room left to write in it. I'd say I have about thirty pages left. I scoop it up and begin flipping through it. Glimpses of various entries bring back memories. I close the journal and stare down at it.

As I hold it in my hands, I glance down at the scars that cover my hands and forearms. I've had them for years. I don't remember it happening, but I was told that I was burned the night my aunt and uncle died. There was a fire and I was the only survivor. From the looks of it, I must have moved something that was on fire to escape. They told me I was lucky they didn't get infected, that it could have led to amputation. After placing the journal back in the drawer, I see the other object I've stolen. A large kitchen knife, lying there in the drawer. Having it around makes me feel a little safer, though I'm not certain I'd ever use it. If it were an emergency and I was desperate, perhaps.

I pick the knife up and examine it. I stole it from the kitchen about a month or so ago. That's when some odd things began to happen in this place. So far it hasn't been anything too unsettling...but I don't know how bad it might get. Sybil told me last night that she thinks there may be a Shadow running amok around here. She thought I was that Shadow when she attacked me. I hide the knife back in the drawer and lie down on my bed. I suppose this is the part where I tell you something about myself. Something most people aren't aware of. Even Annie doesn't know. Not yet anyway. I'll be fetching her within the hour. I did promise her that she could meet Sybil. My parents used to refer to Sybil as my "imaginary friend", something that frustrated me to no end. She's made it clear that she's real and no one can tell me otherwise.

"Wendy?" says a voice from nearby. I sit up to see Sybil standing near the door.

"How much longer must I wait for you?" she teases, "I thought you'd have come to visit by now."

"What are you doing here?" I demand, "I told you, I'll come to you from now on."

"What are you getting so worked up about?" she groans, "No one can see me unless I want them too."

"You almost got caught last time," I growl, "Go back to the Plains and wait for me there."

"I'm not going back without you," she insists, "It's boring without you around." We both hear footsteps in the hall and turn to face the door. My heart skips a beat as Melissa walks back into the room, a look of frustration on her face.

"Looks like I'll need your help with this after all," she says, "Can't find anyone who's not busy at the moment. So, if you don't mind, I'd appreciate you helping me move my things."

"I see you haven't done anything with that knife," Sybil mutters. I grit my teeth and try to pretend that Sybil isn't there.

"Not a problem, Melissa," I smile. We both pick up a box and head out into the hallway. Sybil follows after us, muttering the entire time.

"Why are you helping her?" Sybil grumbles, "I thought you hated her?"

"In here," Melissa grunts, gesturing toward her new room. She pushes the door open with her foot, "Just set it on the bed." Sybil follows us back to the room where one large box remains. Melissa and I each grab one end and carry it to her new room. We set it on the floor and as

I turn to leave, I almost collide with Sybil who is standing just behind me. Melissa notices my sudden stop and gives me a strange look.

"Something wrong?" she asks.

"No, not at all," I assure her, heading into the hall as I speak.

"Aside from that she's still breathing," Sybil mutters.

"Thank you...I guess," Melissa mumbles, closing the door behind me. I wait until I'm back in my room to speak with Sybil. I close the door and turn to face her.

"What on earth do you think you're doing?" I snap, "This is why I tell you to wait on the other side. I don't care if it's boring. You made me look like an idiot just now."

"Calm down," Sybil moans with a roll of her eyes, "I was only trying to have a little fun."

"Why were you going on about killing her?" I demand.

"I don't like the way she treats you, plain and simple," Sybil replies, smoothing out her dress, "I don't care for that red-haired woman either," she adds, "What's her name? Favela?"

"I don't like them either," I groan, placing my hand over my face in frustration, "but don't you think it's up to me to decide how I deal with them? Your solutions are always so...extreme."

"Yours are too soft if you ask me," Sybil grumbles, "If they weren't around to bother you, wouldn't that make things better?"

"If they were to be murdered, there's an off chance they may end up in your world," I argue, "I'd rather visit you without having to deal with a murderous ghost or two."

"I wouldn't let them harm you, you know," she assures me.

"That's not the point!" I snap, "Just let me deal with things my way. When I want your advice, I'll ask for it."

"The thing is you never ask for that sort of advice," Sybil laughs, "but I know you want to." She winks at me and giggles.

"You're tiring to be around sometimes," I moan.

"Where's that Annie girl?" Sybil asks, seating herself on Melissa's old bed, "I thought you said I could meet her?"

"I'm not so sure that's a good idea after the things you've been saying."

"From what you've told me, she sounds very nice," she continues, "I won't do anything, I promise."

"You'd better be on your best behavior," I warn her, "I won't tolerate any nonsense from you."

"You have my word, Wendy."

Chapter 3

I've known Sybil since I was three years old. She's much like an older sister to me. She took care of me for a while after my parents died. That was just before I came to Red Oak. She told me she used to live in the same house as me, but I'm not sure if that's the case. As I continue toward Annie's room, I'm doing my best to avoid getting caught by any of the night staff. Sybil agreed to stay in my room and wait for me to return, but it took a great deal of convincing.

I know I said before that the Plains are a sort of...middle ground. A place that's between the safety and calm of the Oasis, and the torment and chaos of the Abyss. Similar to this world, there are places that are more dangerous to be in the Plains, as well as areas that are safer. The same way that walking into a war zone would be considered a dangerous place here, and something like your own home would be considered safe. Most people in this world know Shadows as "Shadow Ghosts." To most others, they appear as humanoid silhouettes, masses of dark energy that often avoid people. Though some prefer confrontation.

Again, similar to the living world, most Shadows are decent enough. Some are cruel and wicked, others kind and friendly. Sybil is sort of a mix between the two. She can be cold and cruel, but warm and caring when she chooses. I have reason to suspect that she and some other Shadows may be to blame for what's been happening around here. I don't buy her story of the lone vigilante on the prowl for troublesome Shadows. My guess is that she led some other Shadows here and they got out of hand. I imagine she was planning to capture them and kick them out before I could find out. I plan on speaking with her about it later. For now, I need to fetch Annie.

I can see her room up ahead. A large number twenty-three riveted to the outside. Once I reach the door, I give it a few light knocks. I hear Annie telling the other wards that she'll get the door. I give one final glance down the hall, just to be certain I don't get caught. The last thing I need is another lecture. Especially from Miss Favela. Just the thought makes me roll my eyes. The door creaks open and Annie peeks out.

"Oh, hello Wendy," she smiles, glancing out into the hallway, "Where's that friend of yours?"

"Sybil? She's back in my room. I'd rather we don't keep her waiting."

"Wendy, I don't mean to be rude," she begins, "but it strikes me as odd that she isn't with you. Are you certain that this isn't some sort of trick?"

"It's like I said before, Annie," I explain, "She doesn't live here. I felt it best that she stay hidden in case I was caught. Can you imagine the trouble I'd be in if one of the staff were to discover her?"

"I suppose that makes sense," Annie admits, stepping into the hall.

"Are the two of them going to keep their mouths shut about this?" I ask, referring to her two roommates.

"Oh, of course," Annie scoffs, "Don't worry, they won't be a problem." She shuts the door and we head down the hallway.

"So, what's Sybil like?" Annie asks, "You said before that she could be worse than Melissa."

"Yes, if she weren't my friend," I reply, "Trust me, she's very nice. Though, you may want to brace yourself before you meet her."

"Why's that?"

"I'm not sure how to put it," I explain, "She's just...different."

"How so?" Annie inquires, "Are we talking about appearance or personality?"

"I'd say her appearance may shock you more than anything," I explain, "Just be ready for it."

"Is she disfigured in some way?"

"Not really," I answer, "Just don't scream, okay? I don't want us waking up half the building."

"You're starting to scare me," Annie replies, "I'm beginning to wonder if I should be taking this with more salt than usual."

"Are you saying you never take anything I say seriously?" I tease.

"Well, you are pretty sarcastic much of the time," Annie replies, "A little over-dramatic and prone to exaggerating as well."

"I appreciate your honesty, but there's no need to wonder if I'm telling you the truth or not. You're my friend, Annie. I would never lie to you."

"I'm not calling you a liar," Annie protests, "It's just that...well..."

"Well, what?"

"Just forget it," she grumbles. Once we reach the door to my room, I poke my head inside. Sybil is nowhere to be found. I roll my eyes and push the door open.

"It's like she enjoys making me look like an idiot," I growl as Annie follows me inside.

"I thought you said she was waiting for you here?" Annie says, seating herself on Melissa's old bed.

"She must have wandered off," I grumble, "I can't believe her. I told her to stay put. She never listens to me."

"Well, we'd better go find-" Annie begins.

"About time you came back, Wendy," Sybil grumbles, stepping into the room. Annie turns pale and collapses onto the bed. Sybil laughs and closes the door behind her.

"I like her already," Sybil giggles, sitting down beside Annie.

"This isn't funny, Sybil," I scold, "You scared her half to death." I walk over to Annie and begin trying to revive her.

"It's not like I hurt her," Sybil protests, "Why can't I have a little fun? I laugh when things happen to you all the time. I have yet to hear you complain about it."

"It's different when it involves my best friend," I mutter.

"I thought I was your best friend?" Sybil pouts.

"You both are," I say, "No reason we can't all be best friends." I shake Annie a little and she lets out a muffled groan.

"I suppose that's true," Sybil says.

"Maybe this was a bad idea," I sigh, "Even if I can wake her up, she'll just pass out again the second she sees you. Or worse, scream and run away." I look back at Annie and resume my efforts to awaken her.

"How's this?" Sybil asks from behind me.

"How's what?" I turn to face her and my eyes widen in surprise. Her scleras have become white rather than her usual black. Her skin looks much less pale, and for the first time I can see color in her cheeks. Her clothes are no longer stained with blood and her black aura has vanished. One final detail remains. Her irises are still red.

"Better," I say, still somewhat taken aback, "Much better."

"Good," she smiles, "Now maybe I won't give her a heart attack."

"I'd say there's much less chance now," I reply, "Although, your eyes might bother her."

"What do you mean?"

"They're still red," I explain, "Last I checked, the living had no such eye color."

"Fine," she groans. She closes her eyes and re-opens them, "How's this?"

"Green is perfect, Sybil," I smile, "Thank you. Never knew you could change your appearance like that."

"Only in the living world," Sybil explains, "Doesn't work in the Plains. Any Shadow can do it." Annie lets out a groan and we both turn to see her sitting up.

"What on earth was that?" she mumbles.

"How are you feeling?" I ask.

"Fine," she answers, "A little dizzy, but fine." She looks up at Sybil.

"Who is she?" Annie asks as I help her to her feet.

"Never mind that," I reply, "First I want to make sure you're okay." Annie wobbles once I let go of her, but otherwise she seems fine.

"Where did that other girl run off to?" Annie asks.

"Sybil is right here," I smile. Annie looks at Sybil, then at me. A look of confusion is plastered across her face.

"I must be losing my mind," Annie mumbles, "I thought she was some kind of...ghost, or a demon or something."

"Demon?" Sybil giggles, "Haven't heard that one before."

"Of course you haven't," I snort, "Annie's the only one I've introduced you to."

"I should have the nurse give me a once over," Annie mumbles, rubbing her eyes, "Can't imagine what caused me to hallucinate like that."

"I promise you, Annie, you weren't hallucinating," I assure her.

"Clearly I was," Annie protests, "I mean, she had red eyes just a moment ago. And the blood, it was all over her."

"I did some cleaning up," Sybil smiles, "Didn't want to scare you anymore than I already did. My guess would be that Wendy didn't quite prepare you, did she?"

"What are you talking about?" she asks.

"She altered her appearance to make you more comfortable," I explain, "I would've suggested it sooner, but I didn't know she could." I give Sybil a dirty look and she smiles back at me.

"Well, that's it then," Annie sighs, sitting back down on the bed, "I've gone mad, haven't I?"

"Yes, this is all just a bad dream," Sybil teases, "You'll wake up soon...maybe..."

"That's not funny, Sybil," I growl.

"Not to you..." she retorts.

"So...why did you bring me to meet her?" Annie inquires, "It wasn't to scare me, was it?"

"No, she just wanted to meet you," I say.

"I don't mean to be rude," Annie begins, turning to face Sybil, "but what are you?"

"A Shadow," Sybil smiles.

"A Shadow?" Annie repeats.

"We call ourselves Shadow Spirits," Sybil continues, "but 'Shadow' is easier."

"I'm afraid that raises more questions than it answers," Annie mumbles.

"You were right earlier," Sybil explains, "When you said you thought I was a ghost. I used to live in Wendy's old house. I met her when she was three."

"So, the blood you had all over you," Annie continues, "What about that?

"About twenty years ago, I had a bit of an accident," Sybil explains, "I used to work in a factory and I was torn up by the machinery." Annie cringes.

"How awful," Annie whispers, "I can't imagine..."

"Ripped my head clean off my shoulders," Sybil giggles, "Lopped off my left arm and gashed me up in a few other places. Not something I'd ever want to do again."

"You sure seem chipper about it," I observe.

"Seventeen-year-olds don't belong in such dreadful work environments," Sybil grumbles, "I'm lucky to have lived that long. Didn't end up in the nicest of places, but I prefer it to five twelve-hour work days a week. At least now I can do whatever I please, and without the constant looming dread of impending death."

"Wow, that was depressing..." Annie mumbles, "Makes me grateful just to be in this less-than-wonderful place."

"I don't know about the two of you," Sybil says, "but I think we've had plenty of time to chat. Let's go have some fun."

Chapter 4

Sybil steps up to the door and places her palm against it. Annie and I watch as a black substance spreads from beneath Sybil's hand and begins to envelop the door. She steps back, smiling while she admires her handy work. The substance engulfs the entire door and frame, turning it as black as night. Sybil approaches the door and pushes it open. A flood of black and white rushes into the room and engulfs all three of us.

"What's going on?" Annie gasps, staring at her hands in horror. She looks at me and lets out a yelp.

"It's alright, Annie," I assure her, "It's part of entering this realm."

"Welcome to the Ashen Plains, Annie," Sybil smiles. I watch as Annie's expression changes from shock to curiosity. She still seems rattled, but not in danger of fainting. Sybil's usual form has returned and both Annie and I have changed as well. Sybil leads Annie to the mirror that hangs over my desk. Annie gasps and clasps her hands to her face in shock. Her eyes are now red like Sybil's with black scleras and her skin has become paper white. My own appearance has been altered in the same way. Even our clothes have changed. What little color they have has vanished, giving way to the black, white, and gray shades of the world around us.

"Come on, Annie," I giggle, tugging on her arm, "Let's go." Sybil leads us out into the hallway. I can see that Annie notices the difference. We're still in the hallway of the orphanage, but it's abandoned and falling apart. Dim rays of light are shining in through the shattered windows. Water drips from broken pipes and puddles on the floor.

"This is so...bizarre," Annie whispers, examining her skin and clothes, "I never dreamed such a place existed."

"It's not great, but it's home," Sybil says as we head into the dining hall, "Not sure why I ended up here, but I guess it's better than the Black Abyss."

"What's that?" Annie asks.

"It's a place that makes this world look sunny and cheerful," Sybil explains, "It's where the most evil souls end up. Most would call it Hell. Here in this place, it's just dull and lifeless. A sort of middle-ground."

"So, is this...like Limbo or something?" Annie asks, "How do people end up here?"

"In a way," Sybil replies, "Like I said, I'm not all too certain about why I ended up in this place, nor do I really know why so many people end up here...rather than upstairs."

"Upstairs?" Annie repeats.

"I've heard it called by a few names," Sybil replies, "Some call it Heaven, but I've heard it's supposed to be full of light and people who I suppose were less terrible than me. Most call it the Glowing Oasis."

"It's easier to call each of them, Abyss, Plains, and Oasis," I add, "That's what I do anyway. Easier to remember."

"I'll keep that in mind," Annie replies, glancing around, "Where are we going?"

"Wherever we want," Sybil replies, "The nice thing about this place is that you'll never find a locked door. Everything is in such disrepair that getting into any building becomes child's play."

"Does anyone ever try to fix anything?" Annie inquires.

"Oh, they try all the time," Sybil giggles, "It's amusing to watch. You'll never find anyone trying to fix anything if they aren't new here. The buildings always return to their original shape the moment you turn away. The same goes for destroying something. Here, let me show you." She glances around and looks at me.

"Wendy, do you know where the stairs are in this place?" Sybil asks, "I can never seem to remember."

"They're just out this way," I reply. I point toward a nearby doorway and lead them out of the dining hall and up the stairs. At the top of the stairs, Sybil spots a large vase sitting atop a small display table.

"Perfect!" she exclaims. She picks it up and carries it to a nearby window.

"Can one of you open this for me?" she asks, nodding toward the window. Annie unlatches the window and pushes it open. It swings outward with an ear piercing squeal. I cringe and cover my ears.

"Okay, now you both see that this is in one piece, right?" she asks us.

"We do," Annie and I chorus. Sybil smiles and tosses the vase out the window. The three of us crowd around the window and watch it shatter on the street below.

"Okay, now back away from the window," Sybil instructs, "Make sure the vase is out of sight." We do as she says, wait a few seconds, then look back out the window. There on the street below, sits the vase. All intact and not a scratch on it.

"How strange," Annie murmurs, "I'm not sure what to say."

"There's one more thing about the Plains that I'd like to show you, Annie," Sybil explains, "If you don't mind, that is."

"Oh, yes, absolutely."

"Okay, for this, I'll need you to stand in front of the window," Sybil explains, "There's a certain point out in the city, a large smokestack along the horizon. I need you to find it and look right at it." Annie squints and stares out across the rooftops.

"Where is this smokestack?" she asks.

"Straight ahead, can't miss it," Sybil assures her. I look at Annie, then at Sybil who has a mischievous grin on her face. She winks and struggles to stifle her giggling.

"This is getting ridiculous," Annie groans, "I don't see any-"

"Bombs away!" Sybil shouts. She grabs Annie's legs and pushes her out the window. Annie screams as she tumbles to the asphalt below.

"Sybil!" I shout. She ignores me and laughs hysterically.

Annie strikes the sidewalk with a thud. I glance out the window to see her getting to her feet. She looks up at us and crosses her arms. I can see that she's trembling.

"Why would you do that?" Annie rages, "What the hell is wrong with you? I thought I was going to die! My God, you're wicked! You're a terrible person!" She kicks the base of a streetlamp in frustration and makes an obscene gesture at Sybil. Sybil laughs even harder and falls backwards onto the floor.

"She's right, you know," I mutter.

"You're just now figuring that out?" Sybil laughs.

"Sorry, Annie!" I shout from the window, "She won't do it again." I turn and give Sybil a dirty look.

"She'd better not!" Annie snarls.

"You didn't get hurt, did you?" I grin.

"I wouldn't be standing if I had!" Annie shouts, "I...um...wait a moment. How am I not hurt?"

"You can't get hurt in the Plains," I reply, "Well, you can, but you can't feel pain."

"Injuries heal up very quick too," Sybil adds. She's now lying on her back, staring up at the ceiling, "Don't forget to tell her that too."

"Come on back up, Annie," I call with a wave. She shakes her head and heads inside through the back doors.

"That was fantastic," Sybil cackles, getting to her feet, "I just hope she doesn't hate me for it."

"I'm sure she'll still be upset when she gets here," I reply, "but she won't be cross for long." Moments later, Annie comes up the steps with her hands behind her back.

"Sorry, Annie," Sybil apologizes, "It was just too good to pass up."

"It's alright," Annie smiles, "I understand."

"You sure you're alright?" I ask Annie. She nods and continues walking toward us, her hands still tucked out of sight. She stops a few feet away, smiling at the two of us.

"You're beginning to scare me," I declare, "Is something wrong?"

"No, not all," Annie replies. In a flash, she leaps forward and plunges a large kitchen knife into Sybil's neck. Sybil stumbles backward and falls to the floor.

"Now she's getting it," Sybil laughs. Annie and I both laugh as Sybil pulls the knife from her neck and examines it.

"Two can play that game," Sybil grunts, crawling her her feet. She hurls the knife at Annie and it pierces her heart. She laughs and pulls it out, then stabs Sybil in the stomach. Sybil laughs and picks another vase up off the floor. She chases Annie down the hall and kicks her down the stairs, both of them laughing the entire time. I catch up just in time to see Sybil hurl the vase down on top of Annie. It shatters into countless pieces. Annie gets up laughing while she brushes herself off. Sybil yanks the knife out of her stomach and clutches it in her hand.

"Congrats, Annie," Sybil says, "You're one of us now."

Chapter 5

Having just left the orphanage, the three of us head down the street. A light breeze is blowing and Annie is taking in the sights. She seems most interested in the few white silhouettes along the street and peppered in various windows. They resemble patches of human-shaped smoke, only lingering for a few moments before fading away.

"Are these people from our world?" Annie asks.

"They are," Sybil confirms.

"Why do they look like this?"

"I'm not sure," Sybil admits, "It's just how it's always been. However, I do know something else."

"What's that?" Annie inquires.

"If you touch one, you'll be able to see what they really look like," Sybil explains, "Watch me." She stands beside Annie and places her hand on the figure's arm. The smoke dissipates and the figure becomes a tall man in a police uniform, watching the darkened city streets. He appears in full color, contrasting against our surroundings. Sybil taps the man's arm again and he returns to his former state.

"That's incredible," Annie whispers, "Do you watch people in our world?"

"All the time," Sybil smiles, "I watch you and Wendy sometimes."

"That's why she wanted to meet you," I explain to Annie.

"Again, I'm sorry for scaring you," Sybil apologizes, "That was careless of me."

"No worries," Annie smiles, "I'm still getting used to all this. It feels like a dream."

"I felt the same way at first," I say.

"I have another question," Annie says, "Why is it that you've never used this as a way to escape?"

"From the orphanage?"

"Yes," Annie replies, "Seems like it would be easy."

"When you enter this world, you have to leave through the same place you came in," I explain, "On top of that, I don't even know where

I would go. As much as I dislike living at Red Oak, I do get a place to sleep each night, as well as plenty of food to eat."

"That's very true," Annie admits, "I never thought about it that way. I guess I just always wished I could see something other than the same old sights, the same people, same everything."

"This is our way to change that," I smile, "Let's go, we've got plenty of time."

* * *

It takes us a little over a half an hour to reach Hampton Park. When we arrive, its appearance is altered the same as everything else. I've only been here twice in the living world. There the grass is green and well kept, cut short and soft enough to fall asleep on. Here in the Plains, the grass is dry and crunches beneath our feet. The fountain in the center no longer sprays streams of water into the air, rather it sits and collects leaves; the statues in its center are covered in moss and grime. The cement walkways are cracked and in disrepair. The elegant iron fence that surrounds the park is rusting and falling apart. The trees are dead and dying, and as with every part of this world the sunlight is dimmed by a thick layering of gray clouds above us. Despite it all, I'd rather be here in this version of the park.

"Wow, this place looks so different," Annie observes.

"Where is everyone?" I ask, "There's always at least a few Shadows around."

"Looks like it's just us today," Sybil smiles, searching a nearby bush, "First we need to figure out where the bow went."

"Bow?" Annie asks.

"An archer's bow," I explain, "There's a game we like to play with it."

"I always leave it in that shed over there, along with a few arrows," Sybil explains, gesturing toward a large shed alongside the restrooms, "Today I left everything in this bush. Since they aren't here, I imagine Franklin took them again."

"Who's Franklin?" Annie asks.

"He's a friend of mine," Sybil answers, "Well...sort of. I guess he's more of an acquaintance. He's not someone I talk to all that much. I just saw him the other day, but most of the time I go a week or more without seeing him around."

"What makes you think he took them?" I ask.

"He and I are the only Shadows who know about them," Sybil explains, "I left them in the bushes so he could find them without having to look in the shed. I keep them in a secret floor compartment so that no one steals them."

"Why couldn't he get them himself?" Annie asks, "You said earlier that there aren't any locked doors here."

"Yes, but he doesn't know about the compartment," Sybil continues, "I like Franklin, he's a nice guy, but I don't know him well enough to tell him that."

"Is that always why you tell me not to look?" I tease, "You don't trust anyone, do you?"

"Nothing personal, I assure you," Sybil replies, "I just don't want to risk someone stealing them."

"I wouldn't take them," I protest, "Not unless we were using them for their usual purpose."

"Well, none of that matters at the moment," Sybil says, "He's not around and I don't know where he is."

"Why don't we go look for him?" I suggest, "Do you know where he might be?"

"Not really," Sybil admits, "Like I said, I don't talk to him much. Although, I have seen him just down the road from here. Over by the old school building." The three of us turn toward the gates and spot a Shadow heading down the street toward us, a young man in his mid-twenties. I can just make out a quiver slung over his shoulder and a bow in one hand.

"Speak of the devil," Sybil laughs, walking toward the gates. Franklin and Sybil both exchange waves and she waits near the bushes outside the gate.

"Not to sound rude, but does everyone here look like a monster?" Annie whispers.

"Monster?"

"I mean the way everyone has red eyes and black scleras," Annie explains, "They almost look possessed."

"Well...yes, they all have those traits," I confirm, "but I wouldn't use the word 'monster' around them. Sybil told me that most Shadows are sensitive about their appearance."

"Got it," Annie replies.

"Sybil's not too worried about that sort of thing," I add, "Just as long as you aren't trying to offend her, she'll just laugh it off." We watch Sybil and Franklin continue speaking with one another. He hands her the bow and quiver and she clutches them in each hand.

"I wonder what they're saying?" I wonder aloud.

"Beats me," Annie shrugs, "Should we go over and see?"

"I'd rather not," I reply, "I don't want to be nosy." Franklin and Sybil shake hands and the two of them make their way over to us.

"Annie, this is Franklin," Sybil says as they approach.

"Hello," Annie smiles.

"Nice to meet you," he replies with a tip of his hat.

"This is Wendy's friend, Annie," Sybil continues, "I just met her today."

"So, Realm Walkers?" he inquires.

"Yeah, I guess so," I murmur, "Never heard that term before."

"It's a living person who possesses the ability to move between the four realms," Sybil explains, "Did I never tell you that?"

"No, I don't think so," I answer, "What does that mean?"

"It's hard to explain," Sybil admits, "I don't know much about it, but what I do know is that there aren't many people who can come here the way you two have. It's a rare gift."

"What about me?" Annie asks, "Does that mean Wendy and I are alike?"

"Of course," Sybil smiles, "That's part of why I wanted to meet you."

"Strange," I reply, "I suppose you learn something new every day."

"All that aside, what do you say we do what we came to do?" Sybil smiles. She slings the quiver over her shoulder and gives a cheerful grin.

"Are you going to stay and visit with us?" I ask Franklin.

"I suppose I could stick around for a while," he shrugs, "Beats wandering around town." The four of us head toward a nearby table and Sybil lays the quiver across it.

"So, what should we play this time?" she asks us.

"How about Shadow Hunt?" Franklin suggests.

"I hate to always be the one asking questions," Annie grumbles, "but what's Shadow Hunt?"

"It's okay, Annie," I smile, "I had to learn too."

"We assign a Hunter, that's the player who uses the bow," Sybil explains, "Then the rest of us become Runners. The Hunter stays in one spot and counts to one hundred. The Runners all break away and find places to hide. The idea is to avoid getting shot with an arrow." She holds one up and gives her usual toothy grin.

"So what happens if we get hit?" Annie asks.

"If you get hit, and it doesn't matter where, you become a Ghost," Sybil explains, "So at that point, you're still in the game, but you've also lost. It's a Ghost's job to aid the Hunter in finding the remaining Runners; but you can't touch the runners. You can however try to slow them down or shout to give away their positions. One other thing, each Runner is allowed the use of any weapons they may come across. Bottles, knives, pipes, anything. If a single Runner can score ten hits on the Hunter, the Hunter becomes a Ghost, and the Runner who struck them down becomes the new Hunter."

"I don't think anyone's managed to do that yet, though," Franklin adds, "Wendy came close to taking Sybil down once, but she got shot before she could get the tenth hit in."

"I'll get her next time," I assure him. I give Sybil a wink and she smirks in response.

"So, we try to avoid being shot and replace the Hunter?" Annie inquires.

"Yep, that's right," Franklin nods, "Whoever is the Hunter by the end of the game is the winner."

"How do we decide who gets to be the Hunter?" Annie asks.

"Most of the time, we had whoever won the last round start off as the Hunter," I explain, "So that would be Sybil."

"Alright," Annie smiles, "Let's get started then."

* * *

Minutes after leaving the park, I remember that I wanted to talk to Sybil. Over the past few weeks, there have been a handful of strange occurrences within Red Oak. One boy said he was pushed down a staircase, the kitchen staff have claimed that pots and pans have gone missing, and several cupboards have been damaged. To top it off, some of the night staff claim they've been seeing what they call "shadow figures" in the halls at night. As we head down the street, I'm trying to decide how best to approach her. Last time, she seemed annoyed that I asked, like she thought I was accusing her of something. I let out a sigh and continue walking.

"Something wrong, Wendy?" Sybil asks. I shake my head.

"No, it's nothing," I lie. I'd rather the four of us just focus on having a good time, rather than risk starting an argument.

"Your expression suggests otherwise," she replies.

"More than just something," I say, "There's a lot going on." Great, what am I saying? I just told myself I wasn't going to do this.

"Oh, I think I know what you're saying," Sybil nods, "You're still concerned about those incidents at the orphanage? Am I right?"

"Yes, I just...look, I'm sorry, I...I don't know what to do about it," I stammer, "Everyone's on high alert over it. It's to the point where we have to be escorted in groups. Of course that awful wretch Miss Favela is loving it. Just another reason to order me around."

"You don't need to apologize," Sybil assures me, "How long has it been now since it started? A month or two?"

"I'd say about a month and a half," I answer, "Maybe longer. I just didn't want to bother you about it after last time."

"I was out of line," she admits, "I don't know. I worried that maybe it was my fault somehow. I thought perhaps someone else was coming through the doorway."

"What do you mean?"

"Well, not all Shadows can come to the living world," Sybil explains, "Every Shadow has the potential to move through the veil that separates our worlds, but it's a skill, something you have to learn. As with any skill, some people are better at it than others. Some may never even figure it out. It's not easy. The thing is, even hours after I've sealed a path to your world it still remains vulnerable, as well as visible to the power of other Shadows. It's sort of like laying bricks and waiting for them dry. Right afterward it might not take much to topple a small brick wall, but wait long enough and it'll require much more force."

"So that means other Shadows could be visiting the orphanage at night?" I ask.

"That's exactly what it means," Sybil nods, "Just out of curiosity, has it been more of the same things?"

"Yes," I confirm, "There have been more thefts and several sightings of Shadows in the hallways."

"Anything else?"

"Yes, one boy said he was attacked," I answer, "I heard him tell the staff he was being followed down the hallway when something grabbed him. He was hysterical, scared out of his mind. It was frustrating that I knew what it was and that I couldn't say anything."

"That's rather troubling," Sybil says, "I'll have a word with Franklin about it later. I don't think he has anything to do with it, but maybe he can can help us out."

"Thank you Sybil. I appreciate it."

* * *

Sybil and I remain silent until we reach the schoolyard. Annie and Franklin have been carrying on a lengthy conversation since we left the park. The entire time, I'm asking myself the same questions over and over again in my mind. Is it worth it to continue coming here? Am I endangering the other wards because of it? I try to think of something else, but it's been difficult to do as of late. I can't stop thinking about the incidents. As the four of us come to a halt, I return to the present.

"Alright, let's get started," Sybil barks, raising the bow over her head, "First, we need to decide where the boundaries are."

"Well, the entire school is in play," Franklin says, "Inside and out, doesn't matter. I think we should expand it down to at least the theater."

"Sounds good to me," I chime in, "It's best to have a large area to spread out."

"Okay, but what four points specifically?" Sybil asks, "The theater is on Alexandra Avenue. Should we just go from there to Cedar Boulevard?"

"How far would you say that is?" I ask.

"I would say maybe three blocks," Franklin answers.

"How far from those points?" Sybil inquires.

"The old Ridgetop Apartments on 11th seem like a good spot," I suggest, "We could go from there down to the end of Fortner."

"Sounds good," Sybil smiles, "Any questions, Annie?"

"Of course," Annie says, "I don't know where any of those things are. How am I supposed to know if I've gone too far?"

"Just remember the street names," I explain, "That's how I learned. 11th, Fortner, Alexandra, and Cedar." Annie takes a moment, her eyes toward the ground while she mouths the names over and over again.

"Alright, I think I have it," Annie says, "Ridgetop Apartments on 11th, the theater on Alexandra, Cedar and Fortner. I'll remember that."

"Alright," Sybil begins, removing an arrow from her quiver, "I'll start counting. You three split up and I'll come find you." She walks to a nearby lamppost and stands facing it with her eyes closed. Annie and Franklin dash in opposite directions. I watch Franklin bolt into a nearby alley as Annie tears down the street and out of sight. I turn on my heel and sprint into a nearby store. The first thing I need to do is get away from Sybil, but I also need to find a weapon. I've never won a game of Shadow Hunt, and that seems to be because I'm always one of the first few to get caught. This time I plan to avoid the same mistakes.

I begin rifling through drawers, searching for something to use. I hurry down one of the aisles and into the back of the store. I notice an ax among a stack of other tools. I snatch it up and hurry toward the back of the store. Sybil is going to be ready to go soon. I'm likely the one still nearest to her. I run down multiple aisles and at last spot an emergency door in the back of the store. I have to take a moment to stop and think for a moment. If I go through it, will it set off an alarm? That would be one of the most idiotic things I could do. As far as I know, no such things exist in this world. I've never thought about it until now. Most things around here aren't in the greatest working order. I think about smashing out the window, but that could cause the same problem.

As I debate what to do, I hear something on the other side of the store. Something just fell over. My heart races in my chest as I inch toward the door. It's faint now, but I can hear footsteps. I push the door open, holding my breath as I do so. To my relief, the door doesn't make a sound. Now's not the time to celebrate though, I need to sneak out while I still can. Chances are she may spend some time looking for clues to my whereabouts. That should buy me some time...I hope. I close the door without making a sound and hurry off down the alley. Each time I come to a window, I duck below it as I sneak by. I keep to the alleyways, making certain to stay quiet. I stop around a corner to catch my breath. That's one thing I wish the Plains didn't have. You still get tired if you exert yourself in any way. If only I could run for as long as I wanted. I'd never let Sybil catch me again.

Gripping the ax, I try to think of a way to use it. Getting close enough to even touch Sybil is going to be difficult. There was a time where I managed to land nine hits, just as Franklin mentioned. I'd been using a kitchen knife at the time. At least with that I could hit her fast. This thing doesn't feel all that heavy right now, but I imagine I'll be singing a different tune when the time comes to use it. One wrong move and I'll make it easy for Sybil to shoot me. Movement in a nearby window catches my eye. My heart skips a beat as I see Sybil on the other side, bow drawn and an arrow ready to fly straight at me.

I let out a yelp as the arrow sails through the window, sending bits of glass all over the pavement. The arrow strikes the head of my ax and ricochets into a garbage can. Had I not been holding the ax the way I was, she would've struck me in the chest. I stumble backward as Sybil hurls a wooden chair through the window and begins to climb out. I race down the alley, desperate to find a way out. A fire escape catches my eye and I jump up to catch the ladder.

To my surprise, it comes loose and slides down, stopping only a few feet above the pavement. Everything else is so rusted, I had expected that it wouldn't budge. I glance over my shoulder to see that Sybil has readied another arrow. I dive behind a large crate just as the arrow sails past me. Without thinking, I throw the ax onto the first platform and race up the ladder. I can see Sybil struggling to pull both the arrows from the garbage can. Once I reach the top of the ladder, I pick up the ax and scramble up the stairs. I reach the second platform and hear Sybil racing to retrieve the second arrow. It won't be long before she makes it onto the fire escape.

I climb higher and higher until I reach the top floor. I glance over the railing to see that Sybil is already on the ladder. I curse under my breath and use the ax to smash out the window. No point in being quiet. I scramble through the shattered window and into the apartment. In the kitchen I spot a knife block. After leaning the ax against the fridge, I race to remove as many knives as I can. Her footsteps are getting closer. She'll be here any second. I pull the last knife from the block and duck into the hallway. I peek around the corner and spot her coming up the last flight of stairs. I move one of the knives to my right hand and grasp the tip of the blade.

Just as she begins to make her way inside, I hurl one of the knives. It misses and bounces off the wall near her shoulder. I throw a second knife and this time it hits its mark. The blade lodges in her leg as she runs for cover. That's one. I'll need to find another way to attack her at some point. I don't have enough knives to make the ten hits, and trying to collect them afterward will only make me an easy target. She doesn't have to shoot me with an arrow, a simple stab will do. I lean out and hurl another knife toward the couch Sybil is behind. I can see her leg sticking out. The knife pierces the fabric, but bounces back and clatters across the wooden floor.

I throw another and it gashes Sybil's throat as she pokes her head up. She yanks it out and throws it back at me. The blade lodges in a nearby cupboard and I throw another two knives. One clips the arm of the couch and strikes the wall, the second sails over the couch and knocks a vase off a table. I look down at my last knife and debate what to do. Should I keep that ax around, or should I just take this knife with me? An arrow pierces the wall beside me and at once I've made up my mind. I slip the knife into my boot and pull the one Sybil threw from the cupboard.

I pick up the ax and race out of the kitchen, dodging another arrow as I go. I hurl the knife at the last second and watch it bounce off Sybil's arm, leaving a nasty gash in the process. That's three. Her wound closes up almost at once and I don't stick around to watch. I crash through the front door and slam it behind me. For a moment I consider going through another apartment, but there's no guarantee I'll find a way out. I rush down the hallway and down the main stairs. I hear the apartment door swing open and strike the wall. Sybil is hot on my tail. I leap over the railing and fall straight toward the next set of stairs. I botch the landing and end up rolling down to the landing. I pick up my ax and stumble down another flight of stairs. There's an emergency exit straight down the hall.

I race toward it as fast as I can, glimpsing the fire escape signs on the wall as I go. I could just jump if I need to, but this will make things easier. As I burst through the doorway, I feel the pit of my stomach drop out. There's no fire escape to speak of. All that's on the other side is another apartment built dangerously close to the one I'm falling out of. I manage to grab the windowsill before I fall, but I can't pull myself up with the ax. I look down and see that the alley is full of trash and other debris. Sure it'd be no big deal to fall down there, but it will slow me down.

I swing the ax up toward the window and shatter it. I throw it up through the window and begin using the wall of the other building to help myself climb up. I clamber inside and fall onto the floor with a thud. I brush the glass from my hair and pick up the ax. Sybil bursts through the door behind me, but she fails to catch herself and falls down into the alley. Racing out the front door, I go toward the main stairs, but instead of going any further, I collapse near them, panting and gasping for air. I'm so worn out that I can barely stand. If I could sweat here I'm certain I'd be drenched. Minutes pass and I begin to wonder if Sybil gave up. No, she wouldn't do that, she's too determined. She's made that clear anytime she targets one of us in this game. I drag myself to my feet and begin heading down the stairs. Once I get to the landing, a let out a scream as an arrow clips the sleeve of my dress and pierces the wall.

I turn to see Sybil smirking as she draws another arrow. I race back up the stairs and this time head to the roof. I crash through the door to the roof and hide beside it. I ready the ax and wait until I hear footsteps. She must think I'm still on the run. I have to work to suppress a laugh. She gets so caught up in what she's doing that she fails to recognize potential traps. As she reaches the top of the stairs, the door swings open and I slam the blade into her stomach, sending her crashing down the stairs. Four hits. Sybil curses and starts back up the stairs.

I bolt toward the edge of the roof and without thinking, I leap from it. The roof of the nearest building comes up quicker than I thought and I only just manage to land and roll without any problems. I race across the roof, glancing over my shoulder for a moment to see Sybil leaping onto the roof behind me. I try to run faster, but I'm starting to get tired again. The edge of this roof is coming up quick. I'll have to jump again. There's no place for me to hide from her up here. I leap from the edge of the roof and land on the next, tripping after standing up from the roll. I tumble across the roof and crash into a chimney.

"I've got you now, Wendy!" Sybil shouts, taking aim. She fires and the arrow bounces off the chimney and skids across the roof. I hide behind the chimney and try to think of something I can do. She's got me cornered and the only way I'm going to get out is to attack her head on. If I can get those six hits in, I'm home free. I race out from behind the chimney as Sybil is retrieving her arrow and slam the ax into her arm.

She stumbles and falls to the ground. I swing it down at her a second time and the blade bounces off the roof. I go for a third swing and clip her leg. Just four more hits. I swing again and this time something else happens. The ax slips from my hands and flies straight over the edge of the building. Sybil is trying to load another arrow though her raucous laughter, but she isn't having much luck. The knife. I have a knife! I remove it from my boot and flee across the rooftop. I spot a large hole and leap into it. I come crashing down onto a wooden floor and tumble across it. Before I can stand up, a loud creaking sound reaches my ears. I freeze in place and listen for it again. I start to stand a second time and that's when the floor gives way. I crash down onto a hard wooden floor and stumble to my feet.

Before I can get far, I hear Sybil following after me. It's only a matter of seconds before she reaches me. Where is the door? Where am I? How do I get out of here? I charge through an empty room and find myself at a dead end. Before I can turn around, I hear Sybil drop down nearby. I stop and hide in one of the smaller rooms. Great, now if I try to break a window, she'll come running straight for me. There has to be a door somewhere. Gripping the knife in my hand I wonder if maybe I can get away with jumping out at her again. My heart pounding in my chest, I wait for something, anything that will signal her presence. She seems to have stopped moving. She must be waiting for me to screw up. All I have to do is take one small step, make the floorboards creak just once, and it's all over. I don't even want to try looking around the corner.

"You're getting good at this, Wendy," Sybil observes, "You only need to hit me a few more times. Come on! Let's see what you're made of!"

"You're trying to distract me, aren't you?" I reply, "You did this last time."

"You make it sound like I don't play fair," Sybil giggles. I jump away from the wall in surprise as an arrow slams into it. Part of the shaft is jutting out just past my arm. Now's my chance. If I'm quick, I can get her while she's drawing another arrow. I leap out from behind the wall and feel an arrow slam into my chest. I stumble backward and fall onto the floor.

"Brilliant..." I grumble, "I swear, it seems like I have the worst luck with this game." Sybil helps me up and I brush myself off.

"You might've had me if you hadn't lost that ax," Sybil laughs.

"Don't remind me," I groan, "That might be the most ridiculous thing I've had happen during this game."

"Regardless, that was an exhausting run," Sybil replies, "I don't think I've ever chased you so far for so long." She smiles and I remove the arrow from my chest. So far, with the exception of Annie, I'm the only one who's never won a round of Shadow Hunt, but I suppose that's not the reason I play it.

"Come on," Sybil smiles, motioning for me to follow, "Let's go find the others."

Chapter 6

An hour later, Sybil and I have separated, but remained somewhat close by. Now that I've been hit with an arrow, it's my job to help her find Franklin and Annie. I'm almost certain that one of them is in the room below me. Right now I'm standing on the roof of another building, not far from where Sybil and I had our showdown. I'm still playing the events over and over again in my mind. It brings a smile to my lips. At least I didn't make it easy for her. Glancing over the edge, I can see a balcony jutting out from the side of the building. It looks to be a ten foot drop. Right now I'm listening for any signs of movement in the apartment below. Just when I'm beginning to become impatient, I hear it again. The creak of a door opening somewhere inside. I leap from the roof and land on the balcony. As I stand up, I spot Franklin rushing into the hallway.

"Found one, Sybil!" I shout with my hands cupped around my mouth, "Over here! He's getting away!" I sprint into the apartment and hear Sybil's rapid footsteps on the roof as I make my way into the hall. I race toward the stairs and stop to glance over the railing. There's no sign of him. As I turn to go down, I feel a pair of hands shove me down the stairs. I let out a yelp and tumble down them before landing in a heap at the bottom. Sybil races into the hall and looks down from the railing.

"Where is he?" she shouts from the landing.

"I think he went in there!" I call to her. I point to an open door near her and she vanishes through it. It doesn't take long before I hear Franklin struggling to fight back. This is the frustrating thing about being a Ghost. You're allowed to shout to the Hunter and follow after the remaining Runners, but that's all you can do. They are allowed to attack Ghosts, including pushing me down the stairs the way Franklin did. If I could at least be allowed to try to slow other players down without having to avoid grappling, then I would feel more like I'm apart of the game.

Whatever the case, I can still help Sybil out in other ways. I'm allowed to bring her arrows back to her, but again that means making myself a target for Franklin. He once picked me up and used me as a shield to avoid being shot. Didn't do him much good though, the arrow went right through me. Either way, it was a memorable moment that had us all laughing. I run to the stop of the stairs and burst through the door. I catch a glimpse of Franklin racing into another room, closely followed by Sybil. I shut the door and begin searching for something to block it. I notice a desk nearby and quickly push it in front of the door. As I finish with my task, I turn to see Franklin running toward the door. I jump up onto the desk and try to make it harder for him to push it. He tries to push me off, but I'm not letting him. An arrow strikes the door between us and he rushes into the back room.

"Damn, I thought I had him that time," Sybil grumbles. She readies another arrow and follows after him. I stay behind Sybil and keep after her at a steady pace. Before I can react, Franklin leaps out from behind a wall and hurls a mallet down the hallway. It grazes Sybil's ear and strikes me in the nose, sending me reeling. One of the other things I can do as a Ghost is take his weapons from him...if I can get to them first that is. Once it's in his hand, there's nothing I can do. I brush past Sybil and give her a nod as I do. She nods back at me. I stop near the corner and wait for Franklin to make a move. Once he jumps out with a screwdriver, I race past him and immediately see where he's getting the tools from. A toolbox is sitting open near the wall. I pick it up and turn to run, but he's blocking my path.

"Now, Sybil!" I cry. He turns and an arrow goes straight through his neck. He stops and lets out a groan.

"Looks like you got me," he chuckles, removing the arrow and handing it to Sybil.

"Alright, you two, let's go find the new girl," Sybil says, "Can't let myself be bested by a rookie, now can I?" Without warning, Annie lets out a shrill cry and leaps onto Sybil's back.

"Where did she come from?" Franklin exclaims. Annie sinks a large hunting knife into Sybil's chest, once, twice, three times before Sybil manages to throw her off. Annie must have been following us the whole time. Sybil is so shocked at Annie's sudden appearance that she can't figure out what to do. Annie bolts around the corner and out of sight. Sybil chases after her, but only manages to allow Annie another shot. Annie stabs Sybil in the stomach and slashes her twice across the cheek and forehead before running off and vanishing once again. It's then that I see that she's managed to push the door open, despite my having barricaded it. Sybil, Franklin, and I all reach the door at the same time, but Annie is nowhere to be seen.

"Alright, let's split up and find her," Sybil says, standing near the edge of the stairs, "Stick close by and yell if you see any-" Sybil's words are cut off as Annie rushes out of the apartment and tackles Sybil. The two of them tumble down the stairs and Sybil's bow clatters onto the floor in front of me. As they crash onto the landing, I see that Annie and Sybil are both fighting for control of the knife. As they struggle, they move near the second half of the stairs and Sybil pushes Annie down them. Annie grabs the front of Sybil's dress and drags her down with her. Franklin and I follow after them.

Annie stabs Sybil in the back as she races back up the stairs. That makes seven hits. Franklin and I move aside as they pass. He and I should have been doing our job, but we're so focused on the fight that we can't look away. Sybil reaches the top of the stairs and Annie leaps onto her back once more. Annie stabs Sybil in the neck and gets elbowed in the nose before she can land another blow. Sybil stumbles to her feet, snatches up the bow and is promptly stabbed again. This time Sybil doesn't try to fight back, she just turns and sprints down the hallway with Annie hot on her heels. She knows that if Annie wounds her one more time, the game is over, and Sybil's reign as champion will come to an end.

Franklin and I run after them and watch as Annie hurls the knife at Sybil's back. Instead of stabbing her, the knife strikes handle first and bounces off onto the floor. It won't count unless she uses the blade. Franklin tries to pick up the knife before Annie, but all he manages to do is catch his foot on it, sending it sliding straight toward Annie. She swipes it up and ducks just as Sybil unleashes an arrow that strikes Franklin in the arm. Annie charges forward, and stabs the knife straight into her chest. Sybil drops the bow and stares down at the knife jutting from her chest. She pulls it out and tosses it aside.

"Looks like we have a winner," Sybil says.

"That also means we have a new Hunter next round," Franklin chimes in.

"I won?" Annie asks through a laugh, "Really?"

"Indeed you did," Sybil answers, picking up the bow, "And like Franklin said, you're our new Hunter next time we play." She hands Annie the bow and then removes her quiver and does the same. Franklin hands Annie the arrow that struck him and she places it in the quiver.

"I've never used a bow in my life," Annie replies, "I'm not sure I should be the next Hunter."

"No worries," I assure her, "We'll teach you to use it."

Chapter 7

"So, back to the park then?" Franklin asks.

"We could just teach her to use it here," Sybil replies, "Why go all the way back to the park for that?"

"Seems better suited for that sort of thing," Franklin explains, "Makes a lot more sense to have target practice there since we have that massive tree available to us. If the arrows miss the target, the tree will prevent them from going too far."

"Won't they just break if they strike the tree?" Annie asks.

"They do sometimes," I explain, "but it's like that vase Sybil threw out the window earlier. If something in this world breaks, it won't stay that way for long."

"Oh, right. I forgot about that," Annie mumbles.

"It takes time to get used to the way things work here," Franklin assures her, "I remember Wendy needing some time to adjust as well." He winks at Sybil and the two of them snicker.

"Why thank you, Franklin for that lovely reminder," I mutter.

"Hey, I didn't bother to mention the ax incident," he laughs.

"True, but that's what you were implying," I grumble.

"The what now?" Annie ask.

"It was sort of like what I did to you earlier," Sybil laughs, "When I pushed you out the window. I chased after Wendy with an ax and tried to hit her with it. She didn't know that pain and injury don't exist here, so she was hysterical the entire time."

"It wasn't funny, you cold-hearted witch!" I snap.

"Relax Wendy," Sybil giggles, "I still remember it plain as day. You were thirteen and I had decided you were old enough to come visit me here. That look on your face when I went running after you was priceless. We had a good laugh at the end, didn't we?"

"You never seem to put yourself in my shoes," I say, "Sure, I laughed out of relief, but before that I thought I was going to be murdered. How is that funny?"

"It's funny because I would never hurt you," Sybil explains, "At least I waited till you were thirteen to pull a stunt like that."

"And that's better somehow?" I snort.

"Better than doing it when you were seven or something," she replies, "Come on, let's get going. I imagine the two of you will need to go back and sleep at some point."

"I don't think we need to worry," Annie replies, "Tomorrow's Sunday. We'll be able to sleep in if we wish."

"At the price of missing breakfast," I remind her, "Those cooks don't wait for anyone."

"I could steal some food for you two," Sybil offers, "Perhaps something that doesn't need to be kept warm?"

"How would you do that?" Annie asks.

"Living people can't see me," Sybil explains, "Not unless I want them to."

"That's kind of unsettling," Annie mumbles, "Can't imagine how uncomfortable I'd be if someone could just watch me go about my day without me noticing."

"She does it to me all the time," I say.

"Not all the time," Sybil counters, "Just...sometimes...I mean...well, I do it to most living people. It's not as though I watch them sleep or anything. Sometimes I listen to their conversations or follow them down the street at night. Just to see where they're going."

"You make yourself sound like a stalker," Franklin teases.

"Tell me, Franklin," Sybil growls, "Are you by chance familiar with the definition of hypocrite?"

"I believe so," he grumbles, "Where are you going with this?"

"It's my understanding that you often follow Breathers around and scare them for fun," Sybil mutters.

"Oh, one time!" Franklin scoffs, holding up his index finger, "It's not as though I made a habit of it. Claire sure did, though. Not anymore, but for a while."

"Claire?" I ask, "That girl I met a few months ago?" Claire was, as I recall, a rather moody girl, about two years older than me with very long hair that reached to her knees. I can never be certain of a Shadow's former hair color, unless it was black. The lack of color in this world can make it difficult to tell sometimes, but I'm certain she had black hair. As for her former eye color, that's anyone's guess. I've never seen a Shadow who didn't have red eyes.

"Yes," Franklin replies, "She's still not accepting of this reality or the fact that she's stuck here."

"I think it's because of the lack of color in this place," Sybil chimes in, "She once told me that she was an artist before she died, and that she loved to paint. We visited her old house one day and she showed me a few paintings that she'd hidden away. I guess her parents thought it was a waste of time, despite how lovely they were. What I'm trying to say is that she used very bright, vivid colors, and she said she misses them."

"That and she can't paint here," Franklin adds, "You can't create, repair, destroy, or dismantle in this world. I've seen her at the art museum in the living world a few times, usually standing around staring at paintings. That seems to be the only time that you can speak to her without having your head bitten off."

"That museum is just down the street," I say, "I wonder if she might know anything about the incidents at the orphanage?"

"Incidents?" Franklin repeats, "What incidents?"

"There have been a few wards at the orphanage who claim they've been attacked," I explain, "The kitchen staff is also up-in-arms over several missing items. Pans, utensils, even one of the brooms have vanished."

"Claire did mention something odd the other day," Franklin recalls, "Though I didn't think much of it at the time."

"You mean those vague ramblings of hers?" Sybil asks. Franklin nods.

"What did she say?" I ask.

"If I remember right, she said, 'As Shadows, we crave that which is now lost to us. I am no different. Regardless, there is no reason to torment those who haven't met our fate.' Something like that. She was referring to the living world, of course. Sounded rather hypocritical coming from her, little miss scare Breathers for fun. She hasn't done that in several months, though. I suppose her attitude has changed. She said that after I asked if she was content to stare at paintings and feel sorry for herself all day."

"Doesn't seem all that odd in my opinion," Sybil scoffs, "Sounds like typical Claire to me."

"She's told me that she sometimes visits the orphanage," Franklin explains, "I was frustrated with her at the time and left right after that."

"Why were you frustrated with her?" Sybil inquires.

"She stands around all day trying to figure out what she thinks she did wrong," Franklin explains, "I want her to be happy. Her brother, Tom is still upset that she won't stop wandering around the living world and he feels abandoned because of it."

"Wendy and I will talk to her tomorrow," Sybil assures him, "We've all done our grieving in some way or another. I'm sure Claire will learn to accept it soon enough."

* * *

After leaving the apartments, we head to the main road and begin walking back to the park. I can't stop wondering if maybe Claire knows something about what's been happening at the orphanage. Despite how depressing she can be, I do like her. It's just that she seems to want to be left alone. So, because of that, I haven't bothered to seek her out. I do agree with what Sybil said, that people need time to grieve, but I don't think speaking with her will be of any harm.

The more I think about it, the more I wish I knew just who it was that's been causing trouble at Red Oak. For a while, I suspected Sybil, despite what I may have told her. She has a history of blathering on about how much she wants to get back at Melissa and Miss Favela. As I've said to her before, I need to deal with them myself. I feel I may have caused some of Sybil's overprotective tendencies by depending on her so much when I was younger. Regardless, I suppose it is nice to have someone who cares about me as much as she does.

"You sure are quiet, Wendy," Annie observes, halting my train of thought. I see that Sybil and Franklin are both walking several feet ahead of us. They seem to be engaged in a deep discussion about something, but I'm only catching bits and pieces of it.

"Sorry," I reply, "Just...lost in thought..."

"How long did it take you to get the hang of this thing?" she asks, holding up the bow.

"To be honest, I still haven't quite learned to use it," I answer, "Not as well as Sybil or Franklin anyway."

"That's encouraging," Annie grumbles, "I think I've guaranteed myself a loss the next time we play this game."

"Why do you say that?"

"Well, if I can't hit anyone, then what good am I as a Hunter?"

"You don't have to be the Hunter next time," I explain, "You can choose someone else to take your place."

"I suppose I could do that," she replies, "Though, I'd rather practice this before I give up on it. Speaking of which, how are you three planning to teach me?"

"Target practice of course," I say.

"Somehow I don't think inanimate objects are involved," she laughs, "Am I right?"

"Sybil or Franklin will stand by you and teach you how to hold it and everything," I explain, "Then myself and whoever isn't helping you will act as your targets. If you want to be an effective Hunter, you'll need to practice hitting moving targets."

"That's not going to be first is it?"

"No, we'll stand still for you at first," I reply, "I may take a turn once you're finished."

"This day is getting more and more strange," Annie says, "At least now I'm feeling less out of touch with reality. However, it still seems surreal."

"I felt that way for months," I reply, brushing my hair away from my face, "Trust me, this isn't a dream."

"Even if it were, it still beats our usual routine at Red Oak," Annie continues, "I suppose I need to stop over thinking everything." She glances at Sybil and Franklin, then back at me.

"What do you suppose they're talking about?" she asks.

"Claire, I assume," I yawn, "I think all that running tired me out."

"Strange we can get tired in a place like this," Annie observes, "I even noticed Sybil and Franklin panting. Do they sleep as well?"

"Never asked," I admit, "I always assumed they didn't."

"I happened to notice a fellow lying on a bench earlier," Annie recalls, "He was turned away from us though, so I couldn't tell if he had his eyes closed. I suppose that wouldn't prove he was sleeping, though."

"True." I kick a pebble toward the sidewalk and watch it bounce around before turning my attention to Sybil and Franklin.

"So, I wanted to ask, who's this Claire you were all talking about?" Annie asks, examining the bow as she speaks.

"I don't know her all that well," I admit, "She isn't around much. She just came to the Ashen Plains about ten months ago. She and her brother both. I'm still not sure why. Neither of them seem to be injured."

"I noticed that with Sybil," Annie says, "Her neck looks like someone stitched her head back on."

"That's because they did," I explain, "She said that she watched them do it. Anyway, this Claire girl...I was hoping she and Tom would be around today. They're both very nice, and if Claire can eventually pull herself out of her perpetual bad mood, it would be great to have her and Tom around more often."

"Tom's her brother right?"

"Yes," I answer, "He and Franklin are good friends, and even though they haven't been here long, I suspect that Franklin has a thing for Claire."

I glance ahead to see that the park is now only a few hundred feet away. I notice movement out of the corner of my eye and turn my head to see two Shadows speaking in front of a building. Neither of them seem to be paying attention to us. I remember that Sybil once told me that I shouldn't tell people that I'm alive. Right now, only Franklin, Tom, Sybil, Claire, and a few others know that I'm a Breather; their word for a living person. Realm Walkers aren't always welcome here. The one good thing I have going is being able to look like a typical Shadow. I haven't discussed this with Annie just yet, but I get the feeling that she's too street smart to spout off about such things. What it comes down to is that we're visitors in the afterlife, and not everyone here is as nice as Sybil and the others. This is the middle realm after all, the people here could have been complete jerks in life, but still not evil enough to deserve a trip to the Abyss.

When Sybil first told me about that, I wondered why it would be a problem. It's not as if they could hurt me if they found out. She did however remind me that it's not beyond a Shadow's capability to go to the living world. Once there, they could harm me the same as anyone else. I still worry that someone might journey to the living world and see me walking around after having visited the Plains, and thus put two and two together. Sybil claims that it would never happen. Shadows don't care enough to put so much time and effort into making sure that

Realm Walkers stay out of their world. They have their own problems to worry about.

Chapter 8

I can see Annie and Sybil about one hundred feet from where I'm standing. We just arrived in the park a few minutes ago and haven't wasted any time in preparing to teach Annie to use the bow. Franklin is several feet to my left, preoccupied with a few stones that he's attempting to juggle. We're both standing in front of the massive tree that sits in the center of the park. Where it stands in this world, there is a large group of smaller ones in the living world. Trees like this one don't exist anywhere but the Plains.

Looking up at it, it must be over twelve-hundred feet tall and two hundred feet wide. The bark is multicolored with swirls and stripes of varying shades of gray, white, and black. Many shades of leaves cover its dozens of branches. The leaves have always been one of my favorite things about these trees. Every so often, a few of them will drift to the ground. They're each large enough for me to stretch out on. This is the only one I've ever seen, and the only one in the city. An arrow whizzes past me, strikes the tree, and bounces onto the ground. I glance down to see that the impact split it in two. Franklin and I both look at it for a moment, then turn our attention away from it. When I look back down, the arrow is back in one piece. If only it was this easy to fix something in the living world. I look up to see Annie readying another arrow. Sybil is standing next to her, pointing at me.

Annie lets the arrow loose and this time it grazes my shoulder. The arrow snaps on impact and returns to normal seconds later. I can't see either of their expressions, but judging from Sybil's body language, she seems pleased with Annie's progress so far. By this point in my training, I was lucky if the arrow went in the right direction.

"She almost got you that time," Franklin chuckles, continuing to juggle his stones, "Not bad for a beginner."

"I was just thinking the same thing," I reply. Just after the words cross my lips, a third arrow flies toward us and strikes Franklin in the arm. Two of his three stones fall to the ground and he lets out a groan.

"Oh, come on," he laughs, "I was doing great that time." I hear Annie and Sybil laughing and I can't help but smile. Franklin pulls the arrow from his arm and tosses it between us. Just off behind the two of them, I see a Shadow walking toward us. It takes me a few seconds, but I recognize him. It's Tom, Claire's older brother. I haven't seen him in weeks. I wave and he waves back. Franklin is so occupied with his juggling that he fails to notice. Sybil and Annie both turn and wave to him.

"Wendy!" Tom calls out, "Might I have a word with you?"

"Certainly!" I shout back. I run toward Tom and feel an arrow collide with my head. It knocks me off balance and I fall to the ground in a heap. I can hear everyone laughing as I stand up and pull the arrow out. I walk over to Annie and hand it back to her amongst her fit of giggles.

"So, you wanted to speak to me?" I ask, turning my attention to Tom.

"Yes," he replies, "It should only be a moment. I don't want to take up too much of your time."

"You could always join us, you know," I suggest, "I'm certain everyone would love to have you around."

"I'll think about it," he replies, "By the way, who's the girl that just shot you?"

"Oh, that's Annie," I reply, "She's like me. We're here visiting and it's her first time being here."

"I see," he says. He glances at Annie, then back at me, "Two Walkers in the same town, huh? What are the chances?" he continues as we head to a nearby bench, "I thought you were the only one. Too bad I'm not just a visitor here. I wish Claire and I both were."

"Is she what you wanted to talk about?"

"Yes," he confirms, "I wanted to know if you've heard anything. Franklin does his best to keep me informed, but I thought I'd ask if you'd spoken to her."

"I'm afraid I haven't," I admit, "Not since the last time we were all together." We plop down on the bench and watch the others.

"How long has it been since then?" he asks, "Do you know?"

"Two months at least," I answer, "I know it was in April, but I'm not sure of the exact day."

"It's not important," he assures me, "It just seems like much longer than that. I suppose it should considering the way time works here. I still haven't figured out how much slower it is here."

"I think it's twice as slow," I reply, "I usually come here for a few hours at a time. By the time I leave only half that has passed in the living world."

"Sounds about right."

"So," I begin, "how did you know I was here?"

"I didn't at first," he explains, "I just heard from some of the locals that you four were playing a round of Shadow Hunt a little while ago. Someone said they'd seen you heading this way, so I followed you. I found it somewhat difficult to give descriptions of you all. I didn't realize how hard it is to describe a person without the use of colors."

"I can imagine."

"Anyway, I haven't spoken to Claire in a while. Shadows can't stay in the living world for more than a few hours at a time. She has to be coming back here at some point. I just never see her when she does."

"It's funny," I begin, "My perspective of this place is so much different than the rest of you. I look at this place as an escape, somewhere I can go to be with my friends; but for all of you it's something much less pleasant."

"I managed to save one of her paintings and bring it here," Tom says, "Even so, she says it depresses her. I mean...she's happy I was able to save it; it was her favorite...but having it here means that it's void of the colors she wants to see. She considered bringing it into the living world, but there it's subject to the elements, and time itself. Here at least it's safe. So long as no one steals it."

"Has Franklin told you what he's tried?" I ask.

"What do you mean?"

"I mean, what has he tried to say, tried to do, to help Claire move past this?" I inquire.

"Let's see," he begins. He clears his throat and leans back on the bench. "He's tried to tell her that I'm worried about her, tried telling her that she's not in this by herself, that she can come to the living world to visit the art museum whenever she wants...which seems to have backfired; he's tried to get her to leave, which he somehow managed to do only once so far; they walked down the street for a while and had a talk, but he won't give me any of the more specific details. Says she didn't want him to tell me everything she said."

"Sybil and I were planning to speak with her soon," I explain, "Maybe after Annie and I leave. Of course, we'll have to get some sleep before that."

"Sure would be nice if I could still do that," Tom grumbles, adjusting his hat. I suppose that answers Annie's question. I'll have to tell her sometime.

"I'll have to see what we can do about Claire." I watch Franklin run up the side of the massive tree and flip backwards. He lands and Sybil and Annie both clap. Seems they've gotten distracted as usual. I roll my eyes and lean forward with my elbows on my knees, my chin resting on my palms.

"Has Claire always been so moody?" I ask.

"No," he says, shaking his head, "Not since after we died. She used to be much happier, albeit quiet and a little shy. Here it's like she's a different person. I'm sorry if she's been a bother to any of you, I know how tiring she can be."

"I'm not worried about it," I reply, "I don't think anyone else is either. Sybil and Franklin seem to understand."

"I think she used to vent her emotions through her paintings, but now that she doesn't have that option anymore, it's building up."

"We'll figure something out," I assure him, "Would you like to come visit with us for a while? Maybe it would be a good thing to give your mind a rest."

"Sounds tempting," he grunts as he stands up, "I'm not sure, though. Feels wrong of me to go try to have fun while she's off sulking somewhere."

"She won't always be unhappy," I smile, "I don't think it's wrong to try and enjoy yourself. I'm sure this has been rough on you too." He heaves a sigh and glances over at the others who are all looking our way. Sybil waves to us. The others do the same and we both wave back.

"Well," I smile, "What do you say?" He pauses for a moment, lifts his hat and scratches at his head. He places his cap back on his head and looks back at me.

"I suppose I can stick around for a bit."

Chapter 9

Hours later, I find myself lying in my bed at the orphanage. Annie and I returned from our escapades just before eleven p.m. Tom visited with us for a couple of hours, and I was glad to see him feeling better. Annie had so much fun that she wants to go back tomorrow evening. I can't say I blame her. I imagine she'll remain this excited for at least a week. I roll over onto my side and face the wall. Right now, I'm alone in my room. No Melissa to hassle me about my sleep talking, Sybil has gone back to the Plains, and Annie is back in her current room with her two roommates. I didn't go with her, but I do hope she managed to sneak back in without any problems. Knowing Annie, I imagine she was just fine. Tomorrow I need to speak with Mister Sullivan about transferring Annie down to this room. It would make sneaking off to the Plains much easier.

I glance at a pair of picture frames sitting on my nightstand. One is of me and my parents from when I was two years old. How they got me to stay still for that photo, I haven't a clue. Next to it is a photo of me and Annie from just last year. Melissa used to give me grief for it every so often. She would always say it was weird, but I never let her childish comments bother me. Annie has been like the sister I never had. As I lie there, thinking about the day, I remember that Sybil said she would come to see Annie and I in the morning. Franklin mentioned that he may join us as well. We're going to see if we can find Claire at the art museum down the road. Though, now, with all the restrictions that have been set on myself and the other wards, that may be tricky.

Usually anyone fourteen and older can come and go from the orphanage as they please, so long as they abide by a set of rules. That means we must return to check in every two hours, mustn't wander further than a few blocks, and we are required to be back before six p.m. when everyone is to settle in for the evening. The members of this community do a reasonable job at keeping an eye us, though I still feel I don't need it. Either way, it's nice to know that people are looking out for me in the event that something goes awry. With that final thought, I begin drifting off to sleep.

* * *

My eyes flutter open and I find myself staring up at the ceiling. A thin film over my eyes makes it difficult to see at first. After several blinks, everything comes into focus. That's when I realize that something is wrong. I sit up and find my bedroom falling apart and decaying. Leaves are scattered across the floor, the window is shattered, and rain is falling outside. As I sit up, I realize I'm clutching a bottle in my hand. It reminds me of the train dream. I toss it on the floor and see that it's empty. As I swing my feet off the bed I hear it creak beneath my weight. That's when I notice that my clothes are different. I've never had new clothes in my life, but never have they been in a state of such shabbiness. Not only that, they aren't mine. At least...I don't think they are. I've never seen them in my life. I notice my mirror hanging above my desk, tilted to one side and cracked along a corner. A thick coat of grime covers most of it. As I wipe it off, the image of a total stranger begins to appear in the mirror.

I stand for a moment, staring back at what I can't believe is me. I look to be a few years older, my cheeks are gaunt, dark circles beneath my eyes, my hair is filthy and unkempt. It looks thinner and shorter as well, no longer past my shoulders, rather hanging just above them. Again I think of the train dream. I've never had this dream until now. I can't understand why some of the same things are happening. I place my palms on the side of my face, just to be certain that the mirror is telling me the truth. I glance down at the empty whiskey bottle lying on the floor and then at the window.

The rain outside is picking up. I can hear it coming down with even greater force as I approach the window. The courtyard outside is in complete disrepair. The bushes and small trees are dead and dying, grass is growing up through dozens of cracks in the asphalt, and weeds pepper the gardens. I turn away and move toward the door. As soon as I open it, I'm certain that I hear voices. Searching a few of the nearby rooms, I find nothing. No one is here but me. As I make my way down the hall, I realize that much of the building seems to be charred, as though a massive inferno once tore through it. A door slams behind me and my heart skips a beat. A strong breeze is flowing through the hallway. Even so, I continue to shake as my heart races. The dining hall is worse off than the hallway. One of the chandeliers has fallen to the floor, crushing two tables beneath it. The others swing in the breeze and I begin to worry that they may fall as well. Behind a pile of fallen debris, I can see someone sitting against the wall.

"Annie?" The girl looks up and I can see that her face is smudged with ash. Blood stains her clothes and her leg is broken. She stands up and glares at me. She doesn't seem to notice her wounds. Without warning, she bolts from the dining hall.

"Annie! Wait!" I shout, sprinting after her. I follow her out the front doors and chase her down the street. I brush past people as I go, drawing a number of foul remarks. I almost lose her when she darts out in front of a car. The driver shouts at me and I continue straight into a small group of people. I knock one of the women to the ground and keep running. I see Annie in the distance, but now I fear I can't catch her.

Seconds later, I spot her heading through the gates of the local cemetery. I chase after her, but by this point I'm so tired I can barely stand. I lean on the gate and try to catch my breath. I glimpse Annie running between a row of graves and toward a large hill peppered with dozens of headstones. I press on and chase after her, dodging headstones and trying to step where appropriate. I glance up on the hill to see that Annie is staring down at me, her hair soaked from the rain and plastered across one side of her face and over her shoulders.

"Annie!" I call out, "Annie, why won't you say something? Why are you running?" She stays put, still staring as though in a trance. As I get closer, she turns and rushes off again. The grass is slippery from the rain and I'm having a difficult time getting up the hill. Once I manage to do so, I can see Annie a short distance away, still staring at me. I take a moment to catch my breath before heading toward her. The rain is so intense now that I have to shield my face with my forearm. I lower my arm for a moment to see that Annie has disappeared, and in her place is a weathered stone statue. As I approach, I see that it's perched on a stone slab that protrudes outward along the ground. I kneel down in front of it and read the inscription.

Annie Joan Compton
Born - March 10, 1911

Died - July 22, 1927

I sit back on my knees and look up at the statue. It's clear that it's seen some rough times. Right now I'm not sure what to think. Who or what was I chasing? I stand up and examine the statue. It looks just like Annie, though portrays none of her cheerfulness. The expression is lifeless and cold, a far cry from the smile I know so well. Her hands are placed in front of her, a chiseled bouquet of flowers clutched between them. As I continue to stare at the statue, I hear Annie's voice from behind me.

"She'll try to deceive you, Wendy," she growls as I turn to face her, "Don't listen to her! She did this to us!"

She points at me I look down to see blood pouring from stab wounds to my stomach and chest. Blood drips from my mouth and I fall to my knees.

"She's not your friend!" Annie shrieks. I collapse on the grass. Somewhere nearby, I can hear Sybil calling to me.

"Wendy? Wendy, wake up." I blink and everything goes dark. I feel myself coming to and see Sybil standing over me with Annie beside her. I sit up and see that my room is back to normal, everything neat and orderly. No peeling paint and a window without a crack to speak of.

"Annie?" I mumble. I squint from the light coming into the window and shield my eyes. "Why are you here?"

"Why wouldn't I be?" she smiles, "I am your new roommate after all."

Chapter 10

I shoo them both out into the hall and get dressed. They tell me that Franklin is outside waiting. I'm relieved to know that he wasn't in my room while I slept. He may be a Shadow, but he's still a boy. It takes me longer than usual to get ready. I keep replaying that dream over and over in my mind. I know it wasn't real, but I still find it disturbing. My face is still the same as ever, and my jet black hair is as tidy as ever. Soon I become lost in thought, trying to understand what that dream might have meant. Or perhaps it didn't mean anything at all. Looking at the calender sitting atop my desk, I glimpse the date. May 29, 1927. In the dream, that gravestone said that Annie died less than two months from now. I hope it wasn't predicting the future. I let out a sigh and head out into the hall. I'd rather not keep everyone waiting. As I open the door, everyone greets me.

"Hello," Sybil smiles.

"Are you hungry, Wendy?" Annie asks.

"Good morning," Franklin says with a tip of his hat. I notice almost at once that there are other wards in the hallway, so I smile and nod to both Franklin and Sybil. They understand and Sybil gives me a wink and a nod.

"Not quite, but getting there," I murmur, answering Annie's question.

"It's not much, but Sybil and Franklin managed to swipe some bread and fruit from the kitchen," Annie explains, "It's stashed in my old room at the moment."

"I thought you were moving into this one?" I ask, gesturing to the door behind me, "And how have you had time to speak with Mister Sullivan already?"

"I'm set to move my things this evening," Annie explains, "It's also after ten," she continues, "We – I mean I, tried to wake you earlier, but you were out cold." She gives an anxious grin as two wards walk past us. I wait for them to pass and look back at Annie.

"No need to be that careful," I whisper, "I doubt saying 'we' would arouse suspicion. 'We' could be referring to anyone."

"I know," she mumbles, "It's just that the three of us were wandering around earlier and I was afraid someone would catch me speaking to them. The last thing I need is to be sent to have my head examined."

"I wouldn't want that either," I murmur, "For you or myself. Anyway...let's go find that food you mentioned." The four of us head down the hallway, Franklin and Sybil behind us, both laughing and toying with some of the wards in a playful manner. I glance over my shoulder to see Franklin place his hat on an older boy's head. The boy's expression as he speaks to his friend, shifts from delight to confusion. Sybil giggles as the boy grabs at his scalp.

"What's that on my head?" Franklin narrates, "What is that? It feels like a hat...but I'm not wearing a hat. Am I?" Sybil's giggles become louder as the boy's friend begins examining his head. His fingers move through Franklin's hat like smoke. Annie purses her lips, attempting to suppress her laughter.

"It's gone now," the boy says as Franklin removes the hat.

"Strange," the boy's friend replies, "You sure you're feeling alright?"

"Don't give me that," the boy grumbles, brushing his hand over his scalp, "I'm fine."

Annie and I continue to Annie's room at the end of the hallway. As we approach the door, Annie begins giggling.

"If only I could do that," she laughs while pushing the door open, "I would find all sorts of ways to entertain myself."

"It wasn't that funny," I chuckle.

"Then why are you laughing?" Sybil demands. Franklin closes the door behind us. It would appear that Annie's roommates Maggie and Jasper are someplace else.

"Your laugh makes me want to laugh too," I explain, "I don't know why, but it does."

"So, whose head did my hat visit today?" Franklin asks.

"I don't know their names," I admit.

"No worries," Franklin mumbles with a wave of his hand, "I was just curious."

"You missed it earlier, Wendy," Annie giggles, opening the top drawer of her dresser, "They were both giving Miss Favela a hard time." She removes a small bundle from the drawer and hands it to me. I unwrap it to find some cheese, bread, and an apple.

"Thanks, Sybil and Franklin," I smile, "So...what did you two do?"

"Pushed her down the stairs," Sybil replies.

"As much as I would find that amusing, I hope you're joking," I mutter, taking a bite out of the apple as I glare at her.

"I am," Sybil assures me, "We weren't being mean. Well...not too mean, anyway."

"We held the door to her room closed," Franklin explains, "She thought she was trapped, so she climbed out the window. Right as she set foot on the ground outside, we let it creak open a little."

"She was furious," Annie laughs.

"How did you see all of this without Miss Favela noticing?" I ask Annie.

"I was outside while they were holding the door closed," Annie explains, "I hid nearby once she started climbing out the window. She caught her clothes on a nail and fell out onto the grass. Good thing her room is on the ground floor, otherwise that would've turned ugly."

"If she wasn't, I doubt she would've tried to climb out the window," I laugh, taking another bite of the apple.

"She thinks one of the wards is responsible," Franklin chimes in, "Just thought I'd mention that before it gets forgotten."

"I hope she doesn't try to pin this on you two," Sybil realizes, "We didn't really think that one through. Sorry about that."

"No worries," I reply, "I just wish I could've been there to see it."

* * *

After I'm through eating, the four of us head out into the hallway where we decide to walk to the art museum. We're hoping to find Claire there. It doesn't take long however, for us to run into Miss Favela, who still seems miffed about having to crawl out a window first thing in the morning.

"Miss Warland! Miss Compton!" she growls, spotting me and Annie, "Might I have a word with the two of you?"

"What seems to be the problem?" I ask.

"Where have you been all morning, Miss Warland?" she demands, "I didn't see you in the dining hall. You know wards are to be seated by 7am sharp, correct?"

"I was exhausted," I groan, "So, I missed breakfast, what's the big deal? And stop calling me Miss Warland, my name is Wendy."

"Don't you take that tone with me, young lady," Miss Favela growls, "Just because we relaxed the rules today doesn't mean that people aren't still watching for anything out of the ordinary."

"Relaxed the rules?" I ask, "Is that why I've noticed everyone walking around on their own?"

"It was announced yesterday evening at supper," Miss Favela replies, "Were you off daydreaming when Mister Sullivan made the announcement?"

"Yes, I was on a pirate ship with Blackbeard himself, I was," I retort. I hear Sybil and Franklin snicker behind me.

"You need to follow the rules, same as everyone else," Miss Favela snarls through gritted teeth, "If you go and wander off during breakfast or any other meal, then soon other wards will be thinking the same thing. As one of the older children, you need to set an example for the younglings, understand?"

"Yes," I groan.

"As for you, Miss Compton," Miss Favela hisses, glaring at Annie, "Some of the kitchen staff claim they saw you near the kitchen around the time some food went missing."

"I didn't take anything," Annie insists, "I was bringing my dishes up to the counter like everyone else."

"I didn't say you took anything," Miss Favela mutters, "All I'm saying is that I'm going to be keeping a close eye on you. That food costs us money, and thievery won't be tolerated."

"As long as someone eats it, what does it matter?" Annie growls, "You can stalk me all you want, I have nothing hide."

"I'd hardly call it stalking," Miss Favela mutters, "Whatever the case, I hope I don't catch you taking anything. And how do you know it was eaten?"

"Well, that tends to be what people do with food," Annie mutters, "Why else would someone steal it?"

"I don't need your sass, Miss Compton," Miss Favela growls.

"Oh, shut up you self-righteous harpy," Sybil moans, clapping her palm to her face.

"You know she can't hear you right?" Franklin teases.

"And that just breaks my heart," Sybil mutters. She rolls her eyes and places a hand over her heart.

"Let it be known," Miss Favela continues, "that if anything else is reported stolen, we will be escorting the lot of you in groups again, and the others will have you to blame for it. Do I make myself clear?"

"Yes, ma'am," Annie and I chorus. Miss Favela turns and walks off, disappearing up the stairs.

"That's right, back to your cave," Sybil mutters as we all head to the front entrance, "Miserable old witch. I wouldn't be the least bit saddened if she were to burn like one too."

"If that's what you want to go for, I suppose we could make it appear that she's levitating things," Franklin suggests. Sybil swats him on the shoulder and rolls her eyes.

"What am I going to do with you?" she moans.

"I think the question is, what would you do without me?" he replies.

"I'm sure I'd get along just fine," Sybil teases.

"Gee, thanks," Franklin laughs.

"I can't believe that woman," Sybil mutters. She tilts her head back and stares up at the ceiling, "Now I feel bad about stealing that food. It's like her job is to take out her frustrations on anyone she sees fit."

"It's no big deal," Annie assures her, "Things should be fine so long as we don't try something like that again." I push open the front doors and we make our way down the steps.

"We'll be sure not to do it anymore," Franklin assures us.

"I almost want to steal something again, just to prove that she couldn't catch me, even if she tried," Sybil grumbles as we reach the base of the stairs, "If I were alive, I would've stood right in front of her and gladly accepted the blame."

"Me too," Franklin declares, briefly raising his hand, "but I thought you said she couldn't catch you?"

"Yes, that's right," Sybil replies while I push open the gate, "She couldn't ever hope to catch me. Admitting my own guilt is something else entirely."

"The museum is just down this way," I say, pointing down the street, "Should only take a few minutes."

"Sounds good to me," Annie replies, "Although, doesn't the place cost money to enter?"

"It's free on Sundays," I explain, "Or rather, part of it is free. They just don't let you in the back areas without paying."

"Where is Claire usually at?" Sybil asks Franklin.

"She's most often in the front areas," Franklin answers, "Annie and Wendy shouldn't have any trouble." I notice a car coming down the street toward us while we cross to the other side. A dog riding in the passenger seat begins barking at Sybil and Franklin. They both watch as the car pulls away with the dog still barking at them.

"I always forget animals can see us," Sybil murmurs, "I've always loved dogs. Too bad they're uneasy around me now."

The four of us walk up the steps and into the building. It doesn't take us long to spot Claire. Her black and white form contrasts to the many colors in the museum. She's standing a short distance away, staring at a few paintings.

"Claire!" Sybil calls out. Claire turns and glances in our direction. She squints for a moment, then gives a halfhearted wave and turns her attention back to the paintings.

"I don't think she's happy to see me," Franklin says, "I imagine she's still cross with me."

"About what?" asks Sybil.

"About the argument she and I had the last time I was here," he replies, "I'll wait by the door. Try to get her to follow you three outside. I want her to be able to talk to all of us and that can't happen so long as she's in here. There's too many people around for Wendy and Annie to talk to her. It may take some convincing, so don't give up right away."

"Got it," Sybil nods, "I'll see what I can do." The three of us approach Claire and Sybil taps her on the shoulder.

"What do you want?" Claire growls, glaring at us all.

"We came here to talk," Sybil explains, "We're all worried about you. Tom especially."

"There's nothing to be worried about," Claire mutters, "It's not as though I could die a second time."

"Look, Claire," Sybil begins, "I'm not going to pretend I know how you're feeling, but I can relate. I went through the same thing when I first came to the Plains, we all did. I was asking myself all sorts of questions, like why did I end up here? Why was I not good enough for the Oasis? How can I ever learn to live with this? It's hard I know that much; but we're here for-"

"Tell him to stand outside," Claire interrupts.

"Um...what?"

"Tell Franklin to stand outside," Claire growls, "I don't want to be near him right now."

"He's just here because he's worried," Sybil insists.

"Look...I know he means well, but I just don't want him within earshot at the moment," Claire explains, "If we're going to talk, he needs to leave until we're finished."

"Are you at least okay with these two?" Sybil asks, gesturing toward me and Annie.

"Who's she?" Claire asks, nodding in Annie's direction.

"That's Annie," Sybil replies, "She's Wendy's living friend. She's a Realm Walker like Wendy."

"So you can see me?" Claire asks with an eyebrow raised. Annie nods.

"I guess that was a dumb question," Claire sighs, "You've been looking right at me."

"I just met her yesterday," Sybil continues, "but she's very nice. Also, before I forget, Wendy would like to speak with you at some point. If that's alright with you, of course." Claire takes a moment to think. She crosses her arms and stares down at the floor. She takes a deep breath and exhales.

"I suppose that's fine," Claire mumbles, locking eyes with Annie as she speaks, "We can introduce ourselves in a more formal fashion later. I'd rather not make you look like a loon in front of all these people." Annie smiles and gives a subtle nod. Claire returns the smile and turns back to Sybil. Her smile vanishes and she lets out a groan.

"Why haven't you told him to get lost yet?" Claire demands, throwing up her arms in frustration.

"You're lucky I like you, Claire," Sybil mutters. She clenches her fists and walks off. She then makes a brief exchange with Franklin, and after a few seconds he turns and walks out the door. Sybil returns to Claire who grins and tilts her head to one side.

"Thank you, Sybil," she smiles, "I appreciate it."

"Well, at least you said that," Sybil mutters, "Anyway, would you feel comfortable talking with Franklin around later on?"

"We'll see," Claire answers, "I may feel better later, I may not. Just depends on my mood. Anyway, these repeated attempts to convince me to leave the museum are beginning to bother me. Why do you all insist on coming back all the time?"

"Look, I'm just here for Tom and Franklin," Sybil says. She crosses her arms and tilts her head to the side, "If you want to be upset with someone, then take it out on them, alright?"

"I see you're still as oversensitive as ever," Claire mutters, "Why must you insist on taking everything I say as a direct attack on you?"

"I did no such thing!" Sybil protests.

"You just told me to focus my anger on Franklin and my brother," Claire counters, "Why else would you say something like that? I've told you before, I'm not upset with you. I'm sorry if I come across as abrasive, but I'm just in a very bad mood these days."

"It's because you can't paint, isn't it?" Sybil surmises.

"Oh, I can paint just fine!" Claire bellows, clenching her fists, "It's just that I can't look away from the painting once I finish it, nor can I use the colors I so enjoyed! I've gone over this with the both of them time and time again!"

"With who?" Sybil asks.

"Tom and Franklin, you dimwit!" Claire snaps, "Who do you think I'm talking about?"

"Franklin sure got this all wrong," Sybil groans, pinching the bridge of her nose, "He told me that you were much calmer here...that you wouldn't bite my head off."

"Painting was my world!" Claire continues, "It was the only thing that kept me sane, and now I'm stuck like this! Too bad I can't move objects with any sort of precision in this damn world! I would just steal the paint from one of the stores, the canvases, all that stuff, and I would just find a quiet place to paint! This is nothing like I would have expected in terms of an afterlife! Whose brilliant idea was it to plop us into such a bland wasteland? I sincerely want to know! What on earth could have possessed them to believe that a realm such as the Plains needed to exist? I wasn't an evil person! I was a goddamn angel! I never did anything wrong!"

"Would you mind if I asked you something...personal?" Sybil asks with caution.

"I'll decide once you spit it out," Claire growls.

"How did you and your brother die?"

"Hell if I know!" Claire bellows, "All I know is that one day a few months ago, I woke up dead! I'm almost convinced we may have been murdered. What on earth kills two people while they sleep? Poof, done, dead. Just like that?"

"Poison?" Sybil suggests.

"And who on earth would want to poison the two of us?" Claire fumes, "It's not like we had any enemies. That's why I can't quite bring myself to believe it was murder, but I can't think of anything else and neither can Tom."

"What's the last thing you recall?" Sybil asks, "Maybe figuring out what happened will give you some closure."

"The last thing I can remember was Tom and I standing on the balcony of our home," Claire explains, "We were discussing our parents and thinking of running away. It had become clear that they wanted nothing to do with us. Tom started wandering around, ranting about them, and then the next thing I know, I'm waking up in some strange room I thought was our own. Tom was asleep nearby and I thought maybe I'd blacked out again."

"Blacked out?" Sybil repeats.

"It used to happen every so often," Claire continues, "I think it was stress related. I would always forget things that bothered me, that I couldn't cope with...and the only way I know that, is because Tom would always tell me. Like for instance, I don't recall my own Uncle Terry's funeral. I know I was there, though. I remember climbing into the car, I remember arriving and seeing the casket; but that's where it all ends."

"So," Sybil begins, uncrossing her arms, "You assumed the latest blackout was nothing to worry about?"

"Yes, that's right," Claire nods, "So, because of that, I fell back asleep. I was very tired for some reason. I felt weak, like I couldn't sit up even if I tried. I was about to say something to Tom when I fell asleep. After that, I woke up in the Plains. Same room and everything, just...torn apart and destroyed."

"That's very strange," Sybil replies, "I wonder what happened?"

"Your guess is as good as anyone's," Claire murmurs, brushing her hair way from her face, "Too bad there's no way to tell."

"I wouldn't say that," Sybil counters, "We might be able to find something that could tell us."

"It's not important," Claire murmurs with a dismissive wave, "I just want to be able to paint again."

"There's little that can be done about that," Sybil says, "Why don't you come with us for today? I promise we can find something to help put you at ease." Claire takes a deep breath, holds it, then exhales. She stares down at her feet for a moment, lost in thought. At last she looks back up at Sybil.

"Fine..." Claire mutters, "Just today, though. I won't make any promises. If I want to come back here and see the paintings again, I will."

"Deal," Sybil smiles. The two shake hands and step back. Claire takes one final glimpse at the painting in front of her and begins walking to the door.

"Where are you heading?" Sybil asks.

"Outside."

Chapter 11

As we head outside, Claire takes me by the arm and leads me away from the others.

"Where are you two going?" Sybil calls to us.

"You said she wanted to speak with me," Claire replies. She turns and leads me into an alley behind the museum. We head as far back as we can before coming to a halt at an iron fence.

"We should have some privacy here," Claire murmurs, seating herself on a large crate near the fence, "Now...what did you want to speak with me about?"

"It was something to do with the orphanage."

"There's a lot to be said for what goes on there," Claire replies, "I'll need more than that."

"It was about the thefts and attacks," I explain, "Franklin said you might know something about them."

"I do know a few things," she replies, shifting her weight, "I know I've seen a Shadow walking around the place at night. I've never seen who it was, though. All I know is that it was a girl."

"It wasn't Sybil was it?"

"Like I said, I couldn't tell," Claire continues, "I don't visit the orphanage all that often. I just sometimes pass by it. When I'm in the Plains, I stay at my old house, thinking, trying to figure out what went wrong, why I'm here, that sort of thing. It's stupid, I know, but that's what I do. Anyway, when I decide to come to this world, I usually create a portal in my house, then walk down here after that. That's usually when I see her wandering around."

"What did she look like?" I ask.

"Like every other Shadow," Claire snorts, "Red eyes, black and white appearance, that sort of thing."

"I suppose that was a dumb question," I admit, "I forget about that sometimes."

"It's no big deal," Claire replies, "Regardless, I don't think it was Sybil. She's often with Franklin and Tom during the night. I don't see why she would go and cause trouble in the orphanage anyway."

"She's been hanging around the orphanage at night as of late," I explain, remembering my encounter with her the night before, "I don't really know the reason. All I know is that she tackled me and said, 'I'm fed up with you causing trouble around here.' Or something like that. I don't remember her exact words, but it sounded to me like she was hunting someone."

"Did she say anything else to you?" Claire asks with a raised eyebrow.

"She didn't say who she was talking about, but it was dark when she tackled me," I explain, "It's just...well...she won't tell me anything else."

"Strange..."

"What I do know, is she bears a grudge against at least two people there. One is a girl named Melissa, and the other is a caretaker who isn't all too fond of me. Miss Favela is what I call her. I think her name is Serena Favela, but I'm not certain."

"Why is she holding a grudge against those two?"

"She says she hates the way they treat me," I explain, "but so far, I haven't heard of either of them being attacked. I get the feeling that whoever she's looking for isn't alive. I assume it's a Shadow she's after. She's known about the attacks since they began."

"How severe were the attacks?" Claire inquires, crossing her arms, "What happened and who was attacked?"

"I don't know his name," I begin, "but it was one of the boys who was attacked the first time. He was pushed at the top of the stairs. Thankfully he caught the railing and managed to avoid tumbling down them. Regardless, the incident left him shaken. He refuses to go near that staircase anymore. It's a good thing his room is on the ground floor. The second time someone was attacked, it was one of the cooks. She seems convinced that someone threw a small pot at her head. She didn't lose consciousness, but she did receive a nasty gash. Of course, no one is going to blame a ghost for such things. They're convinced that one or more of the wards are responsible. I imagine my name is in the hat at this point. Miss Favela's been on my case ever since things started happening."

"Well, the only other thing I know is that Glenda has been acting strange as of late," Claire shrugs, "I don't know if you've met her."

"I haven't."

"She's a Shadow I met soon after coming to the Plains," Claire explains, "I'd say a few years your senior. When you said that things have been stolen, it made me wonder if she might be connected. I don't know much about her, but I suspect that she steals things from this world. Sort of a coping mechanism, I guess. No idea what she does with them. I know that wasn't her I saw hanging around Red Oak. I'm certain that she has black hair...had black hair. That's the only hair color I can be certain of with other Shadows. I can't say for certain that she's the one stealing things, but I know she's a thief and I know she's admitted to stealing from this area before."

"How can we find her?"

"We'll go find her later today," Claire grunts as she slides off the edge of the crate, "I know where the people she often hangs around with are most of the time. So it shouldn't be hard to find her. I know that she's been seen with some other Shadows. Questionable company if anything. I'm sure you know by now that not all Shadows are as nice as me. I wouldn't be surprised if Glenda knows who our mystery girl is, as well as who might be behind the attacks. I can't make any guarantees and that means for anything. When we find her, you need to stay on guard and be ready for anything. No telling what kind of stunt she might try to pull. Understand?"

"I understand," I nod as we exit the alley, "I appreciate the help."

"No problem," Claire replies. We exit the alley and I see Sybil, Annie, and Franklin standing near a lamppost. I wonder for a moment how Annie must appear to the other people wandering the streets. She probably looks lost.

"Took you long enough," Sybil teases, "I take it you're both through speaking?"

"For the most part," Claire answers, clasping her hands behind her back, "However, there is something I wanted to ask you."

"What is it?" Sybil asks.

"I'm going to need some help finding a certain Shadow," Claire explains, "I figured we'd do it today if possible. Do you have any plans?"

"We weren't planning anything in particular," Sybil assures her, "but I appreciate you thinking of us. Anyway, who's this Shadow?"

"Her name is Glenda Fray," Claire explains, "Wendy was telling me that some things have been stolen from Red Oak, and I have reason to believe Glenda might know something about it."

"What about the attacks?" Sybil inquires, "Do you know anything about those?"

"Only that I saw a Shadow near the building a few times in recent weeks," Claire explains, "I don't know who she is, or what she's up to, or even if there may be a another party involved. Whatever is going on, talking to Glenda is a good start."

"We could go fetch her now if you'd like," Sybil suggests.

"That's up to Wendy," Claire replies.

"We'll have to go back to Red Oak," I whisper, trying to move my lips as little as possible, "The caretakers expect Annie and I to check in every so often. If we go back, they'll just think we're off in our rooms."

"Who are you talking to?" asks a passing man. I jump in shock and look up at him. He's looking at me with a mixture of concern and confusion.

"You can't be serious..." Sybil moans, clapping her hand to her face.

"I...um..." I stutter, struggling to come up with an answer.

"Tell him you're blind," Claire instructs, "Tell him you thought Annie was in front of you."

"Did Annie wander off again?" I ask, "I hate it when she does that. I must look ridiculous." The man raises an eyebrow and continues staring at me.

"Oh, I'm sorry, Wendy," Annie chimes in, taking my arm, "I'm afraid I got distracted. Were you talking to the air again?"

"I suppose I was," I reply.

"Blind, eh?" the man grunts, "Should've known." Sybil and I sigh with relief as the man walks off and heads into a nearby shop.

"I am not going back to that quack," I grumble as Annie lets go of my arm, "He hasn't a clue what he's doing."

"What are you talking about?" asks Claire.

"Dr. Fulmer, no doubt," Annie says, "I remember him."

"Ah yes, her old shrink," Sybil mutters, "I hated that man with a burning passion."

"Why's that?" Franklin asks.

"About five years ago, I was sent to that imbecile because the caretakers caught me 'talking to myself' as they put it, on several occasions," I explain, "So they sent me to see this Fulmer fellow and he tried to convince me that everything wasn't real. Sybil, the Plains, all of it."

"That man was in such denial," Sybil says, "I used to antagonize him for telling her such nonsense, and he still thought she was lying."

"What sort of things did you do?" Annie inquires.

"I once toppled a few books from a shelf," Sybil answers, "They all fell on top of him, and of course he scolded Wendy for it."

"I was sitting in front of him the entire time," I groan, "How on earth could it have been me? It's just not possible."

"Sounds frustrating," Franklin remarks, "I would've walked right out the door."

"Believe me, I wanted to," I reply, "I stayed because Red Oak said I couldn't continue to live there if I didn't undergo treatment."

"How did you convince them to let you leave?" Claire inquires.

"I told him what he wanted to hear," I say with a shrug, "I wasn't going to get anywhere if I kept telling him the truth. That and the brainless oaf would threatened to send me to the asylum if I didn't start taking things seriously."

"A cousin of mine went there once," Franklin murmurs. He shifts his weight and stares at the ground, "The place was terrible. No attempt at helping the people there whatsoever. Took us months to get him out of there. The experience did more harm than good. He was just as sane as anyone else before he went there. After he came out, things were different." He spits on the sidewalk in frustration before cursing under his breath.

"I've heard all sorts of stories about what goes on in that place," Claire says, "Can't say for certain what's fact and what's fiction, but I've heard of some of the patients being forcibly dunked in freezing water to make them settle down."

"They did that to my cousin," Franklin chimes in, "He lashed out at the staff because he was angry that they weren't taking him seriously. Said he was telling them he was fine, but his cries fell on deaf ears. He ran around the place, wreaking havoc and that's what they did to make him stop. Took a few tries to make him stop completely."

"I can only imagine," Claire murmurs, looking up at the sky.

"Well, you don't have to worry, Wendy," Sybil smiles, "As long as I'm around, I won't let anyone take you to an asylum."

"I appreciate it," I smile, "Glad to know I can count on you."

"I hate to break up this heartwarming moment, but maybe we she head back to Red Oak," Claire cuts in, "That is, if we plan to find Glenda."

Chapter 12

The five of us all head back to Red Oak, arriving well within the time period set by the staff. Annie and I check in with one of them and head to the parlor upstairs. As it most often is on the weekends, we find the room to be crowded. Even worse, I happen to see Miss Favela standing nearby.

"Great, she's here," Annie mutters, "Come on, let's go to the fourth floor."

"And get yelled at for being in the classrooms after hours?" I moan, "I'd rather not."

"Who are you talking about?" Claire asks, brushing past me. I turn my back to the rest of the room and face Annie.

"We're talking about Miss Favela," I answer.

"She's standing in the corner, scowling at everyone," Annie chimes in.

"Ah, so that's the woman you mentioned earlier," Claire recalls, "She looks angry. Almost like she's about to pounce on the first person to put a toe out of line."

"That's exactly what she does," I reply.

"Every single day," Annie grumbles, "Come on, let's get out of here."

"That would be best," Franklin agrees, "There are too many people around. We wouldn't be able to create a portal without anyone noticing."

"Well, let's go then," I insist. We head out into the hallway and walk toward the stairs. Franklin stays near the doorway and Sybil and Claire follow after us.

"Is she following them?" Sybil calls out.

"Sort of," Franklin replies, "I can't tell."

"What do you mean?" Claire asks.

"I think she's talking to a couple of the other staff," Franklin responds, "Sounds like she's at least planning on it."

"That's our cue to hurry," Annie mutters. As we hurry to the top of the stairs, Franklin leaves his post and follows the rest of us. We scurry to the top of the stairs and I catch my foot on the top step. I crash onto the floor with a thud and Annie helps me to my feet. I hear footsteps below us and we bolt into one of the nearby rooms. We all file inside and Franklin shuts the door behind us.

"Okay, let's hurry and get this over with," Claire says, placing her hand on the door. Just as before, it begins to turn black and the color spreads until it consumes the entire door. Just outside we can hear footsteps coming up the stairs. Sybil pulls the door open and we rush through it. Annie slams the door behind us and she I breathe a sigh of relief.

"I wonder what she'll think when she searches all the classrooms and can't find us?" Annie wonders.

"Not looking forward to explaining that one," I mutter.

"You could always tell her the truth," Sybil snorts. We laugh and head down the hallway.

"I can just imagine the look on her face," Annie laughs, "I'm almost tempted to try it." As we move further down the hallway, I notice a tall, dark-skinned woman standing against the wall. She's wearing a long black coat and heavy boots. She looks straight at me and gives a warm smile. As we approach, she uncrosses her arms and clasps her hands together in front of her. Her hair, roughly six to seven inches in length, is tightly curled and hangs just above her shoulders. A single stray lock hangs over her forehead, along the outside of one of her eyes. My heart skips a beat when I realize her eyes are completely black. As we pass her, she places a hand on my shoulder and stops me.

"Just the girl I was looking for," the woman smiles. Her voice is deep and smooth.

"Who are you?" I demand, stepping back. Her lips curl into a smile and she crosses her arms. She stares down at me from her greater height. She looks to be a little over six feet tall.

"You can call me Jessica," she smiles, tilting her head to the side.

"What's going on?" Sybil demands as she hurries to my side, "What are you doing here?" she asks Jessica.

"I'm only here to see Wendy," Jessica replies, "I wanted to ask her how she's doing."

"You're not a Shadow, are you?" I ask, stepping back as I speak.

"It's rather complicated. That's another story - for another time. Right now, I'm interested in your story, Wendy Warland."

"How do you know my name?" I demand, acting braver than I feel.

"I know everyone's name," Jessica explains, "It's a...gift, of sorts."

"Or it could just be that you spy on us," Sybil mumbles.

"Sybil Clarence..." Jessica whispers, placing a hand on Sybil's cheek, "How long has it been since I've seen you?" Sybil pushes Jessica's hand away and glares at her.

"Six months or so," Sybil replies, "What does it matter?" I almost jump out of my skin as Claire begins shouting. She storms over to us with the others in tow.

"YOU!" Claire shouts at Jessica, "I saw you that day! You were in the funeral parlor!"

"If it isn't Claire Benson," Jessica smiles, "Good to see you too, darling. What seems to be the trouble? Hmm?"

"I had no idea what was going on!" Claire rants, "I couldn't find my brother! I was scared and somehow I ended up there! And what did I find? Not just you, but my body as well! I thought I was going mad and you just left me twisting in the wind!"

"You still haven't told me what's wrong," Jessica says.

"I want to know why I'm here!" Claire shouts, "You of all people must know something!"

"I have nothing to do with your presence here," Jessica assures her. It's difficult to tell, but Jessica appears to roll her eyes.

"Bullshit!" Claire rages, "You're the one who-" She stops mid-sentence as Jessica slaps her across the face. Claire stares at her, a mixture of shock and anger in her eyes.

"Sorry about that," Jessica apologizes, "It's just that I can't have you speaking of such things in front of the living." She looks at Annie and I with a warm smile, then back at Claire.

"Who gives a damn?" Claire shouts, stomping her foot in frustration, "They're Realm Walkers! They know more than most living people! How could saying anything be catastrophic at this point? It's not like they'd tell anyone!"

"You know the rules, Claire," Jessica replies, "I'm afraid I can't change them."

"Fine..." Claire grumbles, "Maybe now isn't the best time, but you and I need to have a chat at some point."

"How about the funeral parlor again?" Jessica suggests, "Just like old times. I have other business in that part of town anyway."

"I'm sure you do!" Claire snarls, "I'll be there tomorrow evening at five, and you had better show up!"

"Don't worrying, darling," Jessica says with a wink, "I'll be there." She walks a few paces down the hall and turns on her heel.

"Glad to see you're doing well, Wendy," she smiles, "I'll see you later." In the blink of an eye, her body dissolves into a murder of crows. They fly around the hall and and sail straight through an open window.

"Who on earth was that?" I ask.

"I'd like to know that as well," Annie chimes in, "Whoever she was, she gives me the chills."

"Well, she should," Claire grumbles, "I hate that ridiculous smile of hers," Claire continues as we all head down the hallway and into the dining hall, "Smug little roach! If I could kill her I would!"

"That's great and all," I mutter, "but that doesn't answer my question."

"She's the bloody-" Sybil stops her with a slap to the cheek.

"Why does everyone keep hitting me?" Claire shouts.

"You aren't supposed to talk about Jessica's job in front of Wendy and Annie," Sybil growls, "We could get in serious trouble if you were to let something slip."

"Why is this such a big deal?" Claire grumbles, "As I said before, what harm could it do?"

"You know damn well what harm it could do," Sybil hisses, "I don't want to hear another word about it. I understand your frustration, I really do, but now's not the time. Now come on...let's go find this Glenda girl."

* * *

The entire time we're walking along the street, Annie and I are hanging back behind the others. I don't want to admit it, but after our encounter with this "Jessica" woman, I'm feeling a little rattled. It's not just that either. I can't understand why they would keep secrets from me. My mind keeps going over that moment again and again. Why did Jessica want to speak with me? How did she even know who I was? Who is she?

I glance ahead to see that our group is heading into a shady part of town. Shady for the Plains anyway. We've only passed by here twice that I can recall, and both times I would hear shouting and arguing, as well as an occasional scream or the sound of something being broken. One of the doors to the Abyss is in this area, and who knows what lurks beyond it? It's one of the reasons I never liked being here.

The area doesn't look much different from the rest of the city. Everything is decaying and falling apart, as is the norm here. It's the Shadows that hang around here that bother me. I know I don't have much to fear since this world lacks pain and death, but that doesn't mean there aren't other methods of torture that could be used. I've seen plenty of Shadows who seem to have lost their minds; whispering nonsense and staring off into oblivion. Just the thought makes me shudder. It's like I've said before...Realm Walkers aren't liked by everyone. For most Shadows, this is a dreary place of suffering. A place where they have no joy, no family, no sleep, and no relief from their reality. Claire is a shining example of that, but at least she's friendly, even if she is abrasive at times. We head through a narrow alley and into a small courtyard behind several buildings. At once I see three Shadows all sitting near a corner.

"Glenda!" Claire barks. A dark haired girl with a bob cut jumps at the sound of Claire's voice. She stands up and spots Claire.

"Oh...hey Claire..." she murmurs.

"I need to speak with you," Claire declares, "Right now." Glenda looks down at her feet and scratches her head. She glances up for a moment and exhales her held breath.

"Sure..." she mumbles. She and Claire head into an empty alley and out of sight. That's when I get bowled over by a particular Shadow who annoys me more than any other.

"Oh my God, oh my God, it's really you!" the girl squeals while struggle to free myself from her grasp.

"Get off me, Eliza!" I snarl. I kick her off and scramble to my feet. Before I have a chance to get away, she's managed to jump on my back and wrap her arms around my neck. She laughs hysterically as I try to pry her off.

"This isn't funny, Eliza!" I shout, "I'm not kidding around with you! Stop it!" Her raucous laughter ceases and she slides off my back, but continues to hug me.

"Why are you always so uptight?" Eliza whispers in my ear, "I'm just happy to see you is all." She lets go and circles around to face me. She gives me her usual grin before turning to go after Sybil. Sybil's eyes widen in horror and she tries to dodge Eliza, but only manages to stumble and fall. Eliza laughs and pulls her to her feet. She tightly hugs Sybil and picks her a few inches up off the ground.

"I hate you so much right now," Sybil mutters as she's set back on her feet.

"Oh please, you love me," Eliza giggles, "I haven't seen all of you in so long." She spots Annie and wanders over to her.

"And who might you be?" Eliza smiles. Annie opens her mouth to say something, but she seems too unnerved to speak. Several seconds of silence pass before I say something for her.

"That's my friend, Annie," I say. Annie clears her throat and continues her silence.

"Is she always this shy?" Eliza asks. Annie turns her head and blushes.

"No, never," I reply, "I'm not sure why she's being so quiet."

"Well, no need to be shy," Eliza says, "Nice to meet you, Annie." She hugs Annie so tight that I hear the air being forced from her lungs. When she lets go, Eliza steps back, a broad grin across her face. Annie's eyes wander about, avoiding Eliza the entire time. At this point I'm wondering if Eliza is making her uncomfortable.

"Hi, Annie," Eliza giggles, giving a small wave, "Can you say something?"

"Annie?" Franklin asks, "Are you okay?"

"How strange," Sybil murmurs. Annie inhales and exhales, then walks over to me and grabs my arm. She leads me off behind a small building. She stops and leans against the wall before clasping her hands to her face and slowly pulling them down toward her chin.

"Is there something wrong?" I ask.

"I don't know..." Annie says, "I just...I don't know. I can't place it."

"Place what?"

"She looks so familiar," Annie replies, "I think I know her."

"Is that what it is?"

"Yes," Annie nods, "She even acts like her."

"Like who?" I ask.

"A friend," Annie answers, "A friend who died."

"I take it this was before I met you?"

"Yes, but it was only about a year ago that she died," Annie replies, "I met her at the last orphanage I lived in. After I moved to Red Oak, we kept in touch by writing letters back and forth. One day she just stopped replying. Not long after that, her mother wrote me and explained what had happened. Her name was Beth. This, Eliza girl...she could be her twin. It's uncanny. I know Beth had a sister who was somewhere else at that time, but she never said she was a twin. Hmm... I wonder...?"

"What is it?"

"That girl's name is Eliza, right?" Annie asks.

"That it is."

"Hang on a second... I have an idea," she says. She walks out from behind the building with me close behind her.

"Hey! Eliza!" Annie calls.

"What is it?" Eliza calls to us.

"Can you come here for a second?" Annie asks. Eliza grins and walks over to meet us.

"Suddenly not shy anymore?" Eliza giggles.

"Apparently not," I say.

"Never mind that," Annie insists, "I just wanted to ask you something."

"Well, what is it?" Eliza smiles.

"Do you have a sister?" Annie inquires, "A twin sister?"

"That I do," Eliza nods, "Why do you ask?"

"Is her name Beth?" Annie continues.

"Yes, that's her," Eliza answers, "She's my twin. Our parents thought it clever to name us that way. Eliza and Beth."

"I knew it," Annie says, "Like Elizabeth, but taken apart, right?"

"That's right," Eliza beams, "Our parents settled on the name Elizabeth if they had a girl, but since they had two, they split the name between us. Do you know my sister?"

"Yes, I do...did...do?" Annie stutters, "She died about a year ago. I'm sorry I froze up like that, it's just...a swarm of memories came back upon seeing you. I thought you might be Beth at first."

"Well she's off in a neighboring town at the moment," Eliza explains, "If you'd like, I'll let her know you wanted to see her."

"That would be great," Annie smiles. I glance to my right to see a woman who appears to be in her late twenties walking toward us. She's the one I saw sitting with Glenda and Eliza earlier. Her hair is braided and hangs down the middle of her back. She stops nearby and gives us a somber gaze.

"I assume you've got everything worked out?" the woman says.

"Yes, we have," Eliza replies, "No need to worry, Vivi." The woman nods and leaves without saying another word.

"Who was that?" Annie asks once the woman is out of earshot.

"Genevieve," I reply, "She's sort of...moody."

"She seems sad," Annie observes, "Is she alright?"

"I'm not sure," I shrug, "I've never asked. She's a bit scary, to be honest."

"Yeah, don't let the somber expressions fool you," Eliza giggles.

"Why do you say she's scary?" Annie asks, crossing her arms.

"Let's just say that I've seen her when she's mad," I reply. With that, the three of us rejoin the others. I can see now that Glenda and Claire have returned and Sybil, for some reason has a tight hold on Glenda's shoulders and is shaking her in a rage. As we get closer, I can start to make out what she's saying.

"...not what I asked! I told you to spill it!" Sybil snarls.

"She's dangerous, Sybil, you know that!" Glenda snarls, "If I tell you where she is, it'll get traced back to me, then I'll get in trouble."

"I couldn't give a damn about you or your safety right now!" Sybil rages. She lets go and swats Glenda across the face, "I have a job to do!"

"It's not just about my safety!" Glenda fires back, "What about, you know...her?"

"Her safety is my problem! Not yours! I can handle anything that might come her way! So start telling me what I want to know!" She slaps Glenda in the face and glares at her.

"Is this the part where I say 'ow'?" Glenda taunts. Sybil punches Glenda in the nose, sending her stumbling backward. Glenda laughs and kicks Sybil in the shin, which only makes her even more frustrated.

"I need answers from you, Glenda!" Sybil snarls, "Now quit wasting my time!" I turn my head to see Claire, Franklin, and a man who seems vaguely familiar, all approaching us.

"We're trying to give them some space," Franklin explains, "As you can see, we're not having much luck."

"So, she hasn't told you anything?" I ask. I jump as I hear Genevieve's voice just behind me.

"Not quite," Genevieve mutters, "She did tell Claire a few things. It's just that the little wretch is being stubborn. It really is a shame that physical torture isn't an option in this place."

"Yeah, I saw how well Sybil's attempt worked," I sigh, "What did she tell you, Claire?"

"We have a name, but that's about it," Claire says.

"Actually, two names," Franklin adds.

"Oh, that's right, I forgot about Grenda," Claire admits.

"Grenda?" I ask, "Do you mean Glenda, or...?"

"No, I mean Grenda," Claire asserts, "She's Glenda's twin sister. It's confusing to say the least. Anyway, she told us-"

"Claire, I could use you over here," Sybil calls.

"Ugh...fine..." Claire moans, sauntering off, "Franklin, Brian, one of you explain the rest." I glance at the man standing near Franklin. He looks at Franklin and shrugs.

"Do you want to start, or should I?" Brian asks.

"I guess I can start," Franklin replies, clearing his throat, "Alright... so, Glenda admitted that a Shadow named Linda Martinez and her friend Grenda, have been paying visits to Red Oak Orphanage as of late. The problem is that we don't know where either of them are and Glenda is being as stubborn as a mule about it."

"Well, she has good reason to be," Brian chimes in, "Linda is...well, she's dangerous. There could be serious repercussions. Not just for Glenda and I, but for all of us."

"Like what?" I ask.

"She's one of the city's gatekeepers," Brian explains, "She and a handful of others take shifts guarding the gate to the Abyss. Every city has one. She's threatened to throw us in there multiple times."

"So she has a key?" Franklin asks.

"Yes, yes she does," Brian nods, his voice beginning to shake, "I should know. She tossed me in there once before. Me, Grenda, and Glenda."

"I remember that," Genevieve giggles, "I had to come in there and rescue you three. I should've charged you for the favor. Especially that insufferable Grenda. Hmm...or perhaps I should've just left her in there to rot?" She brushes her hair behind her ear.

"My goodness, Vivi, why are you so mean?" Eliza asks, clinging to Genevieve's arm.

"Misery loves company," Genevieve mutters, "If only we had a key. I would toss Glenda in there and let her think for a while. I'm certain she'd have an answer in no time. Unfortunately there would be no point. Finding a key, and the gate, would mean finding Linda first. I don't know who the other gatekeepers are. No one does."

"How do you know that Linda is?" Franklin asks.

"Because I handed my position over to her," Genevieve explains, "I admit that it's something I still regret." She shakes her head with her eyes closed.

"Why did you give up your position?" Brian asks.

"It was too much of a bother," Genevieve says, "I hated all the sneaking around."

"Sneaking around?" Franklin repeats.

"It's all done very secretively," Genevieve explains, "We leave our post at a specific signal. We're not supposed to look back once we leave. That way the other gatekeeper isn't seen. Each of us signals the other from the shadows and waits for the other to leave."

"What's to stop them from looking?" Franklin inquires.

"They hunt you down and throw you into the Abyss," Brian answers with a shudder, "You never come back. It's to preserve the secrecy. If a former gatekeeper ever returns to the gate, it's the same result."

"Exactly," Genevieve nods, "They almost did it to me once. That was after I attempted to make contact with the other gatekeepers. My intent was to inform them of Linda's unacceptable behavior. No gatekeeper should go blabbing about who they are, it was disgraceful. She was clearly unfit for the task."

"They don't take kindly to accusations," Brian chimes in, "Even if there's a good reason for it."

"And it doesn't matter if you're a former gatekeeper or not," Eliza adds, "They'll victimize anyone who questions them." My heart skips a beat as Sybil lets out an angry shriek. I turn to see Glenda bolting down a nearby side-street and Claire chasing after her.

"We could use some help!" Sybil shouts, beckoning for us to follow. Annie and I sprint after her. Genevieve and Franklin follow after us. Claire and Glenda bolt into an alley. Within seconds I hear glass shattering and Claire shouting something incoherent. I turn the corner to see Sybil climbing through a broken store window and Claire picking herself up off the ground. I follow after Sybil with the others in tow, but Sybil and Glenda are so far ahead of us that it's hard to keep track of them. I just manage to catch a glimpse of the two of them hurrying out a pair of double doors and rush after them. They run down the street and past a lone Shadow standing along the sidewalk. As I get closer, I can see that it's Tom. He looks at me with a confused expression and I hear Claire shout from behind me.

"Some assistance would be nice!" Claire calls to him. I don't have time to see if he's following us, but I think I can hear an extra set of footsteps. Sybil catches up to Glenda and leaps onto her back, sending them both crashing to the ground. Unfortunately, they're both so far off that I can't get to them in time. Glenda manages to kick Sybil off and continue into an apartment building. She slams the door behind her and Sybil kicks it open. By this point, half of our group has caught up to Sybil.

Claire, Tom, and Franklin rush by the door and head around the back, presumably to block the other exits. Annie, Genevieve, and I follow Sybil into the building and we catch a glimpse of Glenda on the second floor walkway. The four of us race up the stairs and toward where we last saw Glenda. A door slams somewhere in a nearby hallway. As we head down it, Sybil orders us to each check a different room.

"If you find her, shout for the rest of us!" Sybil orders, throwing open the nearest door. The rest of us split up and I take one room while Annie and Genevieve search two others. Moments later, I hear Genevieve calling for the rest of us. I head toward the door to see Glenda racing past it. I rush out into the hall and sprint after her. As we reach the top of the stairs, I shove her down them and follow after her. She lands at the bottom of the staircase and I leap on top of her. As I'm attempting to force her arms behind her back, I hear Sybil shouting for us to help.

"She's down here!" I shout, "I caught her!" Genevieve races to the top of the stairs and glances down at me, before looking back down the hall.

"Wendy has her!" she hollers with her hands cupped around her mouth, "Come back this way!"

"Sybil just chased her onto the fire escape!" Annie calls out. Genevieve raises an eyebrow and looks down at me and Glenda, then back down the hall.

"Go after them!" Genevieve shouts, "Sybil might need help." I hear Annie's footsteps echoing down the hallway, and soon they fade out. Genevieve glares at Glenda and comes down the stairs toward us. She kneels down and grabs Glenda by the chin. She pulls Glenda's hair away from her face and examines her. After a few moments, she motions for me to let go of Glenda's left hand, and without saying a word, she looks it over.

"What are you-?" I begin to ask.

"Brilliant," Genevieve interrupts, "She got away. For now."

"What are you talking about?" I ask, glancing down at Glenda.

"That's not Glenda," Genevieve murmurs. She stands up and digs her heel into the girl's cheek, "That's her sister. Grenda."

Chapter 13

"You can't be serious! How did...how...when...?" I stammer. Genevieve removes the heel of her boot from Grenda's cheek and takes a step back.

"I should have known they would try something like this," Genevieve grumbles.

"How can you tell which one she is?" I ask.

"Grenda has a few distinct scars on her left hand," Genevieve explains, "That's the only way I've ever been able to tell them apart." She kneels down again and glares at Grenda with a look of intense hatred.

"Nice to see you too, Genevieve," Grenda mutters, "You mind telling your friend to let go of me?"

"Not on your life," Genevieve growls.

"What life?" Grenda laughs, "I'm a Shadow, Genevieve. I'm dead."

"You know what I mean!" Genevieve snaps.

"You know, I was going to tell you where my sister went," Grenda taunts, "but now I'm not so sure. I don't care for that attitude of yours."

"Spare me," Genevieve growls.

"So, now what?" I ask, "Just sit here and wait?"

"Pretty much," Genevieve replies, "That is, unless we can figure out a way to make her talk."

"How about a bribe?" Grenda suggests.

"How does a kick in the teeth sound?" Genevieve growls.

"You're more than welcome to," Grenda replies, "Why don't you give it a try?"

"I'll pass," Genevieve snorts, "It wouldn't have the desired effect."

"So, what sort of bribe?" I ask.

"I was being facetious," Grenda says, "I have no intention of telling you anything." Genevieve lets out a groan and sits on the bottom of the staircase.

"I bet you're steamed," Grenda taunts, "None of this would be happening if you hadn't listened to your idiot sister. Still can't believe she convinced you to pass the key to Linda. She really is dense."

"Shut your mouth!" Genevieve snarls, "I won't have you speaking ill of my sister!"

"I'll speak of her however I wish," Grenda continues, "Your threats are getting old and your sister can rot in the Abyss for all I care." She lets out a cackle and without giving it a second thought, I slam my fist into the back of Grenda's head. Much to my dismay, she yelps in pain.

"What...the...?" Genevieve whispers, staring at the two of us.

"How did that hurt me?" Grenda panics, "That doesn't make any sense! That's impossible!" she howls. I strike her again and she yelps once more. Genevieve stands up and walks over to us. She glares down at Grenda and gives her a swift kick to the jaw. Nothing happens. The three of us wait in silence for what seems like an eternity. Even I'm confused at this point. I've attacked other Shadows before, and not once have they ever cried out in pain. However, there is just one difference. I've never struck a Shadow with my bare fist until now.

All those times that Sybil and I played Shadow Hunt with the others, the rules always stated that weapons were a requirement. Is that why I never hurt the others? Even that doesn't make sense. I shouldn't be able to harm a Shadow at all. It takes me a moment to realize that Genevieve is staring at me. I glance up at her and look away almost at once. She doesn't seem cross, so maybe she doesn't know what a Realm Walker is. Whatever the case, she's going find out soon enough.

"What?" I ask. She breaks her stare and looks away from me. I glance back down at Grenda and feel a surge of anger. I strike her again and she struggles to get free.

"Stop doing that!" Grenda cries.

"How are you doing that?" Genevieve asks. I struggle to come up with a reasonable response, but nothing comes to mind.

"I...don't know..." I answer, "I really don't know."

"Well, don't stop now!" Genevieve exclaims, "Keep it up! We need an answer from her." Genevieve helps me drag Grenda to her feet and I slam my fist into Grenda's cheek. She yelps and struggles to break free. I strike her several more times, and at last she begs me to stop.

"Alright, alright!" Grenda shouts, "Just stop already!"

"Fine," Genevieve growls, "but first you tell us where Linda is!"

"She's across town at the docks," Grenda says, "She's there all the time."

"Are you certain?" Genevieve asks.

"Yes, it's where we're supposed to go if something happens," Grenda explains, "That's where Glenda went. I was just the decoy."

"Wait here," Genevieve instructs as I take her place, "Make sure she doesn't get away. I'm going to go find something to tie her up with. She's coming with us to the docks." With that, she disappears up the stairs and through an open door. I tighten my hold on Grenda's arms as the tense silence persists. Moments pass and I hear Genevieve searching one of the nearby rooms. For a moment I consider making an attempt to get more information out of Grenda, but it's she who speaks first.

"You're not...going to banish me...are you?" she asks with caution.

"Banish you?" I snort, "What? Like kick you out of the Plains?"

"You know that's what I mean," Grenda replies, "Look, I didn't want to be apart of this. Glenda and I were forced. Linda threatened to send us to the Abyss. What was I supposed to do, ignore her? It's not like I can leave the city. Sure there are other cities far enough out, but I could get lost out in those empty fields! I had no other op-"

"Will you shut it?" I snarl, "I'm not going to send you anywhere." Grenda lets out a sigh of relief.

"Please don't tell Linda I snitched on her, my lady," Grenda pleads, "I imagine she won't be thrilled." I spin Grenda around and hold her by the wrists.

"What did you just call me?" I demand. At once, I can see the intense fear spilling across Grenda's face.

"M-m-my apologies," she sputters, "Was I not supposed to say 'my lady?' I've never met you before and I'm sorry but I'm unsure of how to address you properly, please forgive me."

"Are you feeling alright?" I ask. As soon as the question crosses my lips, I feel stupid for asking it. She's a Shadow...I doubt she's taken ill, or even suffered a head injury.

"Yes, my lady, I'm fine, thank you for asking," Grenda murmurs with a bowed head.

"Why are you calling me that?" I ask.

"Calling you what, my lady?"

"That," I snap, "That right there. Why are you calling me 'my lady?' I'm an orphan pauper."

"Oh, my apologies, my lady," Grenda replies, "I think I understand. What name are you going by?"

"My name is Wendy," I insist, "I don't know what you think you're doing, but you must have me mistaken for someone else."

"Yes, yes, I understand, my...I mean, Wendy," she replies with a nervous smile, "I won't bring it up again, you have my word. Although, there's not much I can do about Genevieve...but she must already...no... no, that doesn't make sense."

"You haven't answered my question," I growl.

"I didn't realize it was you, I'm sorry, I didn't mean to ruin your disguise." She claps her hands together and holds them in a pleading gesture before her. After a few seconds, she drops to her knees and lets her arms fall to her sides.

"Please don't banish me to the Abyss," Grenda begs, "Once was more than enough. I never want to go back there again. If I could sleep, I'm sure I'd have nightmares."

"I already told you," I moan, dragging my palm down my face in frustration, "I'm not going to send you anywhere. I'm not whoever you think I am."

"With all due respect Wendy, inflicting pain in a painless existence more than proves who you are. I promise I won't tell anyone of your disguise and I won't ask anymore questions, I swear it." I hear Genevieve coming back toward the stairs and turn to see her carrying a length of rope. She stares in confusion as she approaches us.

"What's her problem?" Genevieve asks. I look down at Grenda who is still on her knees. Her head is bowed and her long, dark hair is obscuring part of her face.

"Stand up," I order. Grenda leaps to her feet and stands in front of me, "Now turn around and place your hands behind you." Grenda does as I ask and Genevieve continues to stare in confusion. I gesture for her to tie Grenda's hands together and she snaps out of her stupor. Once she's finished, she steps back and looks at the both of us. She shakes her head and moves toward the exit, gesturing for us to follow. Once outside, she breaks her silence.

"What's gotten into her?" Genevieve asks while we head down the sidewalk.

"She and I had a little chat," I explain, "That's all."

"Can I speak with you for a moment?" Genevieve asks, "Alone?" I nod and glare at Grenda who cowers and bows her head.

"Try anything funny and I will banish you," I growl. Genevieve gives me a strange look and we move across the street, being careful to keep Grenda in our sight.

"How did you manage to pull that off?" Genevieve demands, "I've never seen a Shadow do what you did."

"Look, I don't even know how I did it," I admit, "All I know is that I scared that little wretch over there into doing anything I ask of her."

"My problem, Wendy," Genevieve begins, "is that as far as I know, there are only four people who can do what you just did. One is Maris, the ruler of all three worlds; here, the Abyss, and the Oasis. The second is Valeska, the ruler of the Plains. Third is Carmen of the Oasis. The last is Queen Lydia of the Abyss."

"And who are they?"

"You can drop the act, Wendy," Genevieve scolds, "I know you aren't really a Shadow." I feel the pit of my stomach drop out. All at once I have an intense urge to run. Genevieve was one of the Shadows who didn't know who or what I am. As a former gatekeeper, there was no telling how she would react.

"I...um..." I stammer.

"Relax, I'm not upset," she assures me, "I know what's going on and you don't need to explain. I just don't understand why you never told me anything. I just about fainted when you managed to get Grenda to talk."

"Sybil was worried you might have a negative reaction," I explain, "I was told to be very careful with who I told." At this point I'm not sure what she's talking about. Does she know I'm a Realm Walker, or is she convinced I'm whoever Grenda thinks I am?

"That's understandable," Genevieve says, "I just wish I'd known sooner. I can't believe I've never put it together before. The way you seem to only be around some of the time, Jessica's strange interest in you, and your ability to harm Shadows. Obviously there was no way for that last one to not give it away, but still."

"How do you know about that?" I ask, "You weren't there when Jessica and I met."

"Claire was telling me about it earlier," Genevieve explains.

"What does Jessica have to do with anything?"

"Really committed to the act aren't you?" Genevieve snorts, "Anyway, this is just what we need. You'll have some extra pull around here. Although, I suppose that could pose a few problems as well."

"What do you mean?" I ask.

"Well, you must be trying to blend in with the other Shadows, right?"

"Yes, that's right," I lie. So, I see I've gotten my answer. She must think I'm someone else. I just wish I knew who.

"If we can capture Linda, we can bring her before the Midnight Council," Genevieve explains, "They'll have to listen to you." I nod and we head back over to Grenda who is looking around nervously. She seems as though she wants to run away. As we head down the street with Grenda leading the way, I wonder what Genevieve meant by "Midnight Council." If I'm to keep up this charade, I can't ask questions that might give me away. I should just count myself lucky that Genevieve seems calmer than Sybil claimed she would be. Maybe it would be best if I fessed up, or maybe tried to find a way to ask without making my ignorance obvious. I try to think back on what Genevieve told us all before Glenda fled from us. She mentioned some of the details about how the gatekeepers operated, as well as their function, but she never mentioned anything about a council. That may be because she thinks I'm someone with authority. Because of that I imagine she's more willing to tell me things no one else would hear.

None of us speak much for at least thirty minutes while we navigate the streets. As we go, we pass by dozens of Shadows. We're starting to come into the busier part of town. If it's this bad now, the docks are bound to be packed. Finding Linda in a sea of black and white is going to be next to impossible. It's hard to tell even a small group of Shadows apart. Maybe that's why Linda hangs out in this part of town. Getting lost in a crowd would be make escape that much easier. We turn onto one of the main roads and duck into an abandoned shop. No one says a word as Grenda pushes the door closed with her foot.

"It would be best to untie me," Grenda insists, "Once that's done we can head back out."

"What makes you think we're going to do that?" Genevieve snorts, "After the trouble you caused us, there's no way I would give you another chance to run."

"Look, I understand your reluctance," Grenda continues, "but if you want to get to Linda, this is what needs to be done. She's got Shadows watching this entire area like hawks. We may have already been seen for all I know. If word gets back to her that I'm tied up and being led to her location, she and her little cronies will hunt us down. I know because I'm one of them. Seriously, you have to trust me on this. I know what I'm doing."

"What do you think?" Genevieve asks me, "Think we should trust her?"

"If she tries anything, she'll answer to me," I growl. Grenda looks down at the floor and clears her throat. She turns around and Genevieve unties her. Genevieve then takes the rope and ties it around her waist.

"Just in case we need it again later," Genevieve explains, finishing the knot. With that, the three of us head back out of the shop and onto the street, Grenda leading the way once more. With none of us saying a word, I begin to wonder what happened to the others. It's been an hour since I've seen or heard from any of them. They may still be looking for Glenda for all I know. I'm beginning to worry that one of them might find us and cause problems for Genevieve and I. Even if Grenda is afraid of me at this point, there's no guarantee that it will stay that way. Preserving the status quo should be my top priority. There's no telling what we may be walking into. I can just imagine Sybil catching up with us and starting an argument with Grenda. I'd like to believe that she has more sense than that, but sometimes she can be rash. Whatever the case, Claire is likely with her, and I'm certain she can keep Sybil in check.

Continuing down the street, I glance around at the surrounding area. I seldom come to this part of town. As the living world changes, so does its reflection in the Plains. I often wonder how this place will look in the distant future. From what I can see, there are at least two new towers a few blocks away. Nearby are a few shops I've never seen before. One of the side streets is torn up and destroyed, and several power poles lean in various directions; their wires blowing in the breeze as they swing above the street. If memory serves me right, the docks aren't too far from here.

"Walk next to me," Grenda whispers, "You're going to draw attention by following me like that."

"How so?" Genevieve asks.

"I told you already," Grenda grumbles, "She's got eyes everywhere. They watch me and Glenda like hawks." I notice two Shadows, a man and woman, glancing at us from across the street. All at once I feel a sense of dread in the pit of my stomach.

"They must have seen Glenda come through here not too long ago..." I whisper.

"If she got away, that is," Grenda replies, "If she did come through here, then that means we need to be all the more cautious."

"How do we know you aren't trying to lure us into a trap?" Genevieve demands as we come to a stone staircase.

"I'm not about to try anything with her around," Grenda grumbles, motioning toward me, "Trust me, I wish I could, but I'm not about to set myself up for another trip to the Abyss." She crosses her arms and shivers while we continue down the stairs.

"Smart move," Genevieve growls.

"Shut it," Grenda snaps. I roll my eyes and their banter ceases. It would seem the shock is wearing off. Grenda is starting to seem less nervous and afraid. We reach the base of the stairs and head straight onto a crowded street filled with Shadows. I feel almost suffocated. I've never seen so many of them in one place. I can feel their stares as we go. Something about this seems off. I can't put my finger on it, but I have a bad feeling.

I can't show any anxiety, any fear. If I do the other Shadows might pick up on it, they'll get suspicious of me, then who knows that will happen? Sybil warned me when I first came to the Plains, she said that Shadows do terrible things to Realm Walkers. She said it was best that I didn't know. If she had told me, she feared I would never visit the Plains again. So I chose to forget about it. That is, until now. With all this recent talk of gatekeepers and the Black Abyss, it just makes me even more nervous. What are the consequences for a Realm Walker if they get caught?

"You alright there, Wendy?" Genevieve asks me. I snap back to reality and glance over at her with a weak smile.

"Yeah," I lie, "I'm fine." She smiles and looks away, leaving me to drift back into my own thoughts. I've never seen fear in the eyes of a Shadow. Not once. Not until I saw that look in Grenda's eyes when she begged me not to banish her. I can't imagine how bad the Abyss must be. They have nothing to fear here. They're dead, they can't feel pain, they can't get sick, they can't get hurt. Unless someone like me comes along. Unless they're cast into the Abyss. Just thinking about it makes me shudder.

"So," Genevieve murmurs, breaking the silence, "What's the plan?"

"It would be wise to wait until we're away from the crowd," Grenda replies, "No telling who might be listening."

"It's too noisy for anyone to hear us," Genevieve counters, "It seems safe enough. So long as we don't start shouting."

"You need to hide before we get there, Genevieve." Grenda instructs, "Linda will know who you are and I'm sure you know how much she despises you."

"I thought you said there were people watching us?" I chime in, "Other Shadows who would report what they see. Wouldn't she already know that Genevieve is around? Assuming that one of them saw us."

"Linda isn't concerned enough to tell her spies to watch for Genevieve," Grenda explains, "She feels like she has more important things to worry about."

"So she doesn't consider me a threat, does she?" Genevieve asks.

"That she doesn't," Grenda nods, "Big mistake if you ask me."

"Got that right," Genevieve mutters. Up ahead there are two large iron gates. Beyond them is the shipyard. It must be where Linda is hiding. From where we are, I can see several large ships, all decayed and rusting in the murky black waters. Some have partially sunk, disappearing into the depths. Massive cranes tower over the area, their long disused hooks waving in the breeze.

"Alright," Grenda begins, "Here's what we're going to do. Genevieve, you go left once you're inside. There should be a small office building about five hundred feet from the gates. Go about a hundred feet past it and turn right. There should be a small two-story structure dead ahead from there. Go straight there and try not to call attention to yourself."

"Is that where Linda is?" Genevieve asks.

"Yes, she is," Grenda confirms, "Sneak up the stairs and wait there. You should be able to hear us talking with Linda. There's a gaping hole in one of the corners, it's near where she usually sits. You should be able to hear everything we say."

"Anything else we should know?" I inquire.

"She keeps the key on a chain around her neck," Grenda explains, "She never lets it out of her sight. Ever. We need to find a way to get it from her without causing a racket. If any of her guards hear anything, they'll come running."

"And what do we do once we have the key?" Genevieve asks as we approach the gates.

"That's up to you two," Grenda replies. The three of us walk past two small groups of Shadows. They must be some of the guards she was talking about. Each of them are glaring at us, the sight of which is unnerving. One of them motions for us to stop and comes to talk to Grenda.

"What's going on?" the guard demands, "Why are these two with you?"

"Linda requested that she speak with them in person," Grenda lies.

"Is that so?" the guard grunts.

"Look, if you want anymore than that, you're going to have to speak with Linda," Grenda continues, "You know how secretive she is."

"I don't think you're telling me the truth," the guard growls. I hold my breath as the other guards surround us. Dammit Grenda...you'd better not screw this up.

"This is none of your concern," Genevieve cuts in, "This is strictly business between gatekeepers. If you continue to deny us passage, then I will see to it that the council deals with you." My heart skips a beat. What on earth is she doing? The guard smirks and walks right up to Genevieve. He looks down at her from his greater height and clears his throat.

"And who are you?" he asks.

"Adrienne Saunders," Genevieve replies. To my surprise, the smirk vanishes from the guard's face.

"Oh, Miss Saunders, I'm sorry," he apologizes, backing away a few paces, "It's just that-"

"That I'm a recluse?" Genevieve snaps, "That people almost never see me? You didn't recognize me, am I right?" she continues, taking two steps forward, "You tell your guards to stand down...now!" The guard nods and waves for the others to return to their posts. I feel a sense of relief as they move away from us.

"Again, you have my sincerest apologies, Miss Saunders," the guard continues as he pushes open the gates, "It won't happen again, I assure you."

"For your sake, I should hope not," Genevieve snarls. The three of us head inside and once we're out of view, Genevieve sneaks off, leaving me alone with Grenda.

"That was a close one," Grenda mumbles, "I've never tried something like this before; bringing people inside the gates. I didn't think he'd be so persistent."

"That was quick thinking on Genevieve's part," I reply, "Way to think on her feet."

"As much as she bugs me, I guess I'll have to at least give her that," Grenda mutters, "Didn't even think to try passing her off as her own sister."

"Her sister?"

"Yeah, that Adrienne woman she mentioned, that's her older sister," Grenda explains, "They look a lot a like, but if you were to stand them next to one another, the differences would be obvious to anyone. Probably a good thing no one sees her around much."

"I thought no one was supposed to know who the gatekeepers were?"

"They aren't," Grenda confirms while we pass by three Shadows sitting around a small fire, "but Adrienne is the Head Gatekeeper. That's a little different. Everyone knows who she is. They know and they fear her. She's the one who hires all the other gatekeepers. As was said before, Linda is only known as one because of that big mouth of hers. To be honest, Adrienne is part of the reason I hate Genevieve so much."

"What do you mean?"

"Well, it's sort of complicated," she admits, "The thing is, Genevieve defends just about everything her sister does. She sticks up for her even when Adrienne is clearly wrong. She's done that when I question Adrienne's idiotic decision to give Linda of all people a key. Making her a gatekeeper was a huge mistake. Now as for Genevieve, she claims to agree with me, but she still adamantly defends her sister's decision to do so. See what I'm saying?"

"So she wants to defend her sister's right to make the decision, but at the same time she knows it was terrible judgment on Adrienne's part?"

"Exactly," Grenda groans, "but it's not just that. She has more pull with her sister than anyone else. Adrienne values her sister's opinion, and I've asked Genevieve to talk to her about Linda countless times, but she refuses to do so."

"Why's that?"

"Because she has no backbone, that's why!" Grenda snaps, "Remember when I said that everyone fears Adrienne? Genevieve is no different. She's a total wimp when it comes to her own sister. She would rather stay out of her way and just let Linda continue terrorizing people, than just talk to Adrienne for two minutes! It's maddening! I don't understand her. She acts like a wimp and walks about most days, depressed and feeling sorry for herself, but when the time comes for her to be brave, she doesn't have a problem doing it...as long as it's not her sister that she's dealing with."

"I heard she rescued some Shadows from the Abyss at one point," I recall, "It seemed hard to believe with how callous she seemed when I first met her."

"My sister and I were two of those Shadows," Grenda replies, "Not a moment too soon either. Lydia found us. She was going to keep us down there."

"Genevieve told me about Lydia earlier today," I remember, "She called her 'Lydia of the Abyss.' Who is she exactly?"

"She's the devil, that's who she is," Grenda shudders, "She's terrifying. She's evil, she's cruel, sadistic, just...no one you want to meet."

"Aren't you at all grateful for what Genevieve did for you?" I inquire, "If someone saved me from a place like that, I don't think I could treat them with disdain."

"I am grateful!" Grenda snaps, "I will never forget what she did for me and my sister, but that doesn't outweigh all the damage she's caused by refusing to confront Adrienne. I know she's tried to take things into her own hands, but it's gotten her nowhere. She has no pull with the other gatekeepers or the council now that she's no longer a gatekeeper. And speaking of gatekeepers..." I glance ahead to see a tall woman with long, wavy blonde hair. One of her eyes is obscured and she's glaring right at us. This must be Linda. Just behind her is the two-story building that Grenda described earlier. Beside her is Glenda.

"Don't try anything funny," I whisper, "I swear to God if either of you try to pull one over on me, I'll hand you over to Lydia."

"If anything happens, it's not my fault..." she mumbles.

"I don't care whose fault it is," I hiss, "You're all going to the Abyss..." Grenda shudders as we approach. Linda uncrosses her arms and steps forward. She places two fingers in her mouth and whistles so loud it leaves my ears ringing. Before either us us can react, we're both knocked to the ground and restrained. My face impacts the pavement and someone binds my wrists together with chains. Grenda and I are then pulled back onto our knees and held in place. Linda grins at us and stands with two guards on either side of her. Glenda cowers just behind them.

"Hello, Wendy," Linda smirks, "I had a feeling you'd be coming to see me."

Chapter 14

As much as I want to blame Grenda for this, I know I can't. She looks even more scared than I am.

"What are you doing?" Grenda demands, "Let us go! Do you have any idea who you just tied up?"

"Of course I do," Linda sneers, "Don't take me for a fool, Grenda." She snaps her fingers and two Shadows leap on Glenda and restrain her the same way Grenda and I were. Glenda screams and tries to fight back, but they quickly overpower her.

"You're a traitor Linda Martinez!" Glenda shrieks as she's dragged toward her sister and dropped on the ground, "You're a goddamn traitor! The council will send you straight to the Abyss for this! You'll rot there for eternity you traitorous witch! You hear me?" Linda lets out a cackle and stares down at us.

"The only ones going to the Abyss are you lot," she laughs, "Don't worry, though. You won't be going alone." She turns and signals to another guard. He nods and motions for someone out of sight to come forward. My heart sinks as I see a group of Shadows escorting Genevieve and the others. Sybil is struggling to get free while she screams and curses. She's thrown to the ground and held there by three guards. Tom tries to kick one of the guards off and Claire attempts to flee but is captured before she can get far. Next to try escaping is Annie, but she's slammed against a wall and pinned before she can run to Claire's aid. There's no sign of Franklin. I just hope he managed to get away.

"Annie!" I cry. She turns and looks at me with fear in her eyes.

"You're in for it now, Linda!" Genevieve shrieks. She breaks free and charges toward her. Linda's two bodyguards rush forward and hold her back until the others drag her away.

"Maris will rip every ounce of flesh from your body for this!" Genevieve screams, "She'll hand you over to Queen Lydia! She'll send you to the Witherlands! You have no idea what you're getting yourself into!"

"I know exactly what I'm doing!" Linda snarls, turning to face me, "Now that I've got you and your little friends, Wendy, things will be that much easier for me."

"What are trying to do?" I demand, "What do you want from me?"

"Let's just say I'm doing someone a favor," Linda answers, "You'll understand soon enough. Unfortunately, I still have work to do. Once I toss you into the Abyss, Adrienne Saunders is next."

"Go ahead and try it!" Genevieve snarls, "She won't make it easy for you!"

"Formidable as she may be, she won't see me coming," Linda taunts.

"You didn't capture Franklin!" Genevieve growls, "He's on his way to warn her as we speak." Linda's smile fades and she approaches Genevieve with a murderous look in her eye.

"He may not be here with you, but I will find him soon enough," she hisses, "I can promise you that much. There are unseen forces at work here. Things I know you've overlooked. You can shout all you want...it won't help you in the end..."

"This won't stand!" Glenda cries, "The council will send someone after you! They'll banish you!"

"Somehow I doubt that," Linda snorts.

"I didn't even do anything!" Glenda snarls, "Let me go!"

"You attempted to help Genevieve remain undetected," Linda growls, "Don't think I didn't see you earlier! You're no more innocent than anyone else we've captured."

"You're wrong!" Glenda protests, "Grenda and I did what you told us to do! We brought Wendy to you!" I clench my fists and grit my teeth. I knew it. Grenda was lying. I'm willing to bet she taunted me and Genevieve knowing full well what would happen. It was all an act. They planned this from the beginning. But why would Glenda try to assist Genevieve?

"Lying isn't going to change my mind, Glenda," Linda hisses, stooping down in front of her, "I know what happened and you can't change facts." She and Glenda glare at one another for several tense seconds. Glenda spits in Linda's face and she recoils in disgust.

"Take them away," Linda growls, wiping her face, "I've had about enough of them." Each of us are dragged to our feet and herded toward the docks.

"You lied to us!" Glenda screams, "We trusted you!" One of the guards secures a strip of cloth over her mouth. Even so, she continues to let out muffled shrieks. Linda moves to the front of the group. She removes a chain from around her neck and plucks a small black orb from it. That must be the key.

"It doesn't end here," Sybil growls from behind me, "We'll be back, Wendy. I swear it..." I hope she's right...I hope we do come back. I've never been to the Abyss. The things I've heard are enough to send me into a panic. I can feel myself sweating as my heart pounds against my ribs. Once at the docks, we're led down the largest of the many piers and between two massive ships. One of them I recognize from before, back when I could see the shipyard from the hill outside the gates. Just the sight of them both half sunk in the black water is enough to give me chills. I'm half expecting something horrible to crawl from inside them. I shudder as we continue to a large platform at the end of the pier.

We all come to a stop on the platform and Linda holds the key in her outstretched palm. A black, smokey energy rises from it. The orb grows to the size of an apple. The energy fades and without warning, it bursts into a ball of purple flames. Linda removes her hand from beneath the orb and it remains floating in the air. Several seconds pass and the orb shoots out across the water. It stops about two hundred feet away. Beneath it a whirlpool begins to form, and soon it has grown to remarkable size. From the depths of the whirlpool, a large, solid black gate rises to the height of the docks. The gate is decorated with human bones from top to bottom. The edges catch fire in the same elegant purple as the orb moments before. The orb seats itself in a large hole on the front of the gate and it slowly opens.

More purple flames shoot forth, leaving a trail across the water. The flames cool and vanish to reveal a cobblestone walkway leading from the gate to the platform. The others and I are unchained and led down the path. Most of us, including myself, struggle to get away, but it's all in vain. We're outnumbered and there's nowhere to go but through the gate. I can't see anything beyond it except an impenetrable darkness.

"This isn't over, Linda!" Sybil shouts, "I'll make you regret this!" Linda laughs and gives a taunting wave as Sybil and I are pushed through the portal. Everything goes silent and I feel like I'm drowning. It's as though the darkness itself is filling my lungs. There's a sensation of falling and nothing else. I can't see or hear. I can feel myself speeding up, falling faster and faster. I scream at the top of my lungs, but there's no sound. The darkness engulfs my consciousness and for a moment, it feels as if I've ceased to exist.

* * *

All at once, my voice and senses return. I sit up in a panic and my eyes come into focus. As I glance around, I begin to wonder if I'm asleep. Maybe it was all just a nightmare. I'm sitting in an empty train compartment, a massive grassy field peppered with trees is speeding past the window. Seems I have my answer. This is the same dream I've had many times before. With my heart still racing, I stare out the window for a moment. I don't notice anything unusual. The compartment, the scenery outside, it's all the same. There is one difference. I know where the train is going...

"Home," I whisper, "I'm going home." I'm going back to Cinder Valley, the town where Red Oak is. I'm going back, but where was I? None of this makes any sense. My mind is racing, trying to make sense of it all. How can I remember something that never happened? I begin searching my person for anything that might give me a clue. In my coat pocket, I find a train ticket. As I examine it, I realize the city the train departed from is blurred. I glance at the window again and squint at my reflection. I can't make much of it out at first, but as the light adjusts with the passing trees, I see the face of an older me. I look down at my clothes and see that they match the dream from before. The dream where I chased Annie to the cemetery.

"Lovely afternoon, isn't it?" says a familiar voice. My heart skips a beat. I look away from the window to see Jessica sitting across from me. She smiles and tilts her head to the side.

"What are you doing here?" I ask, "What's going on?"

"You remember me," Jessica smiles, "That's good. I was afraid you might forget."

"It'd be hard to forget someone like you."

"Tell me..." Jessica continues, "Do you remember any of this?"

"I remember seeing it before, yes," I confirm, "That's only because I've had this dream before."

"Well, I'm talking about before that," Jessica replies, "Before the dreams began."

"How is that even possible? There's no way I could remember a dream before ever having it."

"Is it a dream?" Jessica says, "Or...could it be something else?"

"I've never ridden a train before," I argue, "There's no way this could be a memory!"

"Then why do you remember it so well?"

"I don't!" I protest, "It's a dream!"

"Have you explored other possibilities?" Jessica inquires.

"Like what?"

"It's my understanding that Claire doesn't know how she got to the Plains. She doesn't know what killed her."

"What does that have to do with me?" I ask.

"In the museum, she told Sybil that she has periods of time she can't recall," Jessica explains, "Do you remember?"

"How do you know about that?" I demand, "Were you watching us?"

"Just answer the question, Wendy," Jessica orders. A tense silence fills the compartment. I sit glaring at her for several seconds.

"Yes," I answer, "I remember. She said she had blackouts. Periods of time she doesn't remember...because of trauma. Wait...no...no that can't be right!" I gasp, "There has to be another explanation!"

"I'm afraid there isn't."

"What about the dream I had before?" I inquire, "The orphanage. Was that a memory too? Did something happen at Red Oak?"

"You have to remember that for yourself, Wendy," Jessica explains, "I can guide you, but I can't carry you. It's a path you alone must walk."

"Don't you understand the position this puts me in?" I quaver, "How can I know what's real and what's not? What about Sybil and the others? Am I just seeing things?"

"Sybil and the rest of your friends are plenty real," Jessica assures me, "The Abyss is very real as well. Your life is very much at stake. You're going to wake up soon, so I'm afraid we need to wrap this up. When you do, find your friends. Make sure they are all accounted for. Leave no one behind. Everything will fall into place from there." She stands up and opens the compartment door. She pauses for a moment and looks back at me.

"One more thing, Wendy," she continues, "I know your sister looks quite a sight, but don't be afraid of her when she finds you. She could be a useful ally."

"What are you talking about?" I demand as I stand up, "I don't have a sister. I'm an only child."

"Are you sure about that?" Jessica smiles. She turns and walks out the door and closes it behind her.

"Hey!" I shout, "Wait a minute!" I open the door and rush into the hallway, but there's no one around. What's going on? As I return to the compartment, the train shakes violently and I'm thrown to the floor. I try to get up, but I lose my balance. The shrill sound of twisting metal and shattering glass fills the air. A deafening crash echoes through the compartment. I slam into the wall and everything goes dark.

I'm drifting back into consciousness. I have to blink a few times before my vision comes into focus. I can see a large, bloodstained chandelier gently swinging from the ceiling above me. My left hand feels wet and something is dripping on it. I sit up to find that it's covered in blood. Not my own, but the blood dripping from the chandelier. I wipe it on my dress with disgust and glance around at my surroundings. I appear to be in an abandoned house. I can see an upstairs balcony and a railing that has been partially demolished. The room is dark and it's difficult to see. A dim light is shining in through a nearby window, but it's not enough to see everything. I head to the window and glance out through the damaged blinds. The light is coming from a streetlamp outside. Looking up at the sky, I can't see anything. It's nothing more than a veil of darkness.

Something crashes behind me and I turn to face the direction I heard it. After a few moments I start looking for an exit. I have a feeling that someone, or something, might be in here with me. It takes me a few moments, but I manage to find the front door. It's locked and I can't get it to budge. I take a step back and stare at the doorknob. I know that locking doors is impossible in the Plains, but here it must be different. I hear something moving around in the nearby kitchen and freeze in place. I hold my breath, waiting for someone to come out. The noises stop and I turn my attention back to the door. I need to get out of here fast. Something crashes again and I start to panic. I kick at the door again and again. It starts to give way, but before it does, a shrill scream echoes from behind me. I turn to see a middle aged woman charging at me with a crowbar. I scream and dive out of the way as the crowbar impacts the door, sending it swinging open.

The woman turns and raises the crowbar over her head. Her eyes are wild with fury. I back into a couch and fall onto it. I dodge another swing and the crowbar smashes into the back of the couch. Before she can swing at me again, I sprint out the front door and into the street. As I go, I pass a number of people, their forms illuminated in the dim light from the streetlamps. Some are fighting with each other, others are sitting against buildings wailing with sorrow, and still others try to grab me as I pass by. I stumble into an abandoned shop and take refuge behind an empty crate.

I'm starting to get scared. When I dodged the woman's first swing, I nicked my arm on what I think was glass. I look down to see that I'm bleeding a little. Not only am I bleeding, I can feel the pain from the wound. This is nothing like the Ashen Plains. The rules here are very different. Here there is pain, blood, and who knows what else? I start to wonder if I could die in this place. Would I just come back? Or would that be the end for me? Jessica said to find my friends, but how am I supposed to do that? And who's this sister she mentioned? For all I know she could've been playing mind games with me. I don't even know if I can trust her yet. Regardless, I do need to find the others. I'm not going to last long on my own.

"You're new here, aren't you?" says a voice from behind me. I freeze in terror. How could I be so stupid? I let someone sneak up on me.

"Um...yeah..." I choke. A woman who appears to be in her late thirties strides past and sits across from me. I lean against the wall, staring at her in terror. Her eyes are sunken and void of warmth. She appears to be missing at least two of her front teeth and blood is dripping from one corner of her mouth. Her long, snow white hair is covered in splotches of blood, as are her clothes. In one hand she's clutching a lantern, and in the other she holds a hatchet.

"Name's Reika," she murmurs, placing her lantern on the floor beside her, "Who might you be?"

"Wendy," I mumble. Reika stares at me with a look of amusement. It's difficult to tell in the flickering light, but I can just make out her blue eyes and pale skin. Judging by her features and attire, she looks to be of Japanese descent, possibly having died sometime in the 1700's.

"So, Wendy," Reika begins, picking at the bloody bandages covering her left hand and forearm, "What did you do to get here? Strange to see someone as young as you in the Abyss. You must've done something terrible."

"I didn't do anything!" I growl, "I'm innocent! I don't belong here!"

"Ha! That's what they all say," Reika laughs. She can't be the sister Jessica told me about...can she?

"I'm serious!" I don't even know why I'm bothering. Who cares what this woman thinks?

"Yeah?" Reika snorts, "Well, I seriously didn't kill my husband." She chuckles and brushes her hair away from her face.

"What?" I gasp. Great, I'm trapped here with this woman as the closest I have to a friend.

"I have to admit, I didn't really think that one through," she grumbles, "I suppose I just snapped. All those years of watching my life travel further and further down hill with each passing day. I imagine that would drive anyone mad. Wouldn't you agree?"

"Why would I?" I snap, "Why are you even telling me this?"

"Why not?" she chuckles, "I love chatting with new arrivals. Anyway, as far as I'm concerned that bastard got what he deserved."

"And it seems you did too."

"I disagree," she hisses, "Some people deserve to die. Some people are wicked, unfeeling monsters. Some people are beyond reason, beyond help. Sometimes survival demands bloodshed...as you will soon discover. So...what's your decision, Wendy? Live or die? Kill or be killed?"

"Live..." I whisper. Reika's stern expression melts away. She grins and lets out a cackle.

"You'd do best to keep that in mind," she warns, "Danger is all around. No telling what you might find or who you might run into. No one else around here will think twice about smearing you along the street. You should get going, Wendy. Can't sit here forever."

"You're right," I grunt as I get to my feet, "I should." Reika giggles and does the same, picking her lantern up as she goes. I try to leave, but she steps in front of me.

"You're not going anywhere...." Reika whispers, "...not without this." She winks and hands me her lantern. My heart is racing as I eye her hatchet.

"Good luck, girly," Reika says, exiting the shop as she speaks, "You're gonna need it." I glance at the lantern for a few moments, then look back at the doorway. Why would she give me this? Why would she want to help me? With a heavy sigh, I venture back out onto the street. I need to find Sybil and the others. First I need to decide where to start.

* * *

For close to a half an hour, I wander the streets, trying to stay out of sight as much as possible. I had a few brief run-ins with some nasty locals since my encounter with Reika. None of those people were any less creepy. I start to wonder if perhaps I should find a place to hunker down and take shelter. It seems like a good idea, but also a terrible one. What if I hide so well that the others overlook me? I'd get left behind in this place. I can't even bring myself to think of what that would be like. On the other hand, moving around could make it even more difficult for the others to find me.

If they're searching as frantically as I am, then who knows how many times I may have already missed one or more of them? The only good thing so far is that I haven't been attacked, at least not in the same way that woman attacked me with a crowbar. There was at least one older man who grabbed me and threw me to the ground. I'm just glad the lantern didn't break. It's proven to be useful. I've managed to find a part of the main streets that's less crowded. I've only passed about a half dozen people in the last few minutes. Most of them were sitting against the sides of buildings, and at least two were scowling at me from upstairs windows. I've been trying to make sense of the streets and buildings, looking for any familiar patterns or landmarks, but so far I haven't seen anything I recognize. I had at first suspected that this place was yet another, more sinister reflection of Cinder Valley; but that doesn't seem to be the case.

I tilt my head back for a moment to examine the upper floors of a motel. Gazing up at it, it's hard not to notice the black sky above me. Not a single star in sight. No moon either. Just darkness. I turn my attention to a group of people walking in my direction. There are three of them, two men and a woman. They all seem terrified, looking in every direction as they go. It's as though they expect to be attacked at any moment. Considering what I've seen in this place so far, that doesn't seem unreasonable. I hear angry shouts coming from the third floor balcony of the motel and watch as two men throw a third over the railing. The man plummets to the street below and lands with a sickening thud. Having closed my eyes just before the impact, I hesitate to open them. Once I do, I wish I hadn't.

The man's leg is bent at an unnatural angle and a bone is jutting out of one of his arms. Blood is spattered on the street near his body and more begins to pool around his head. I look up to see the two men laughing and cheering. They both spot me and an evil grin spreads across each of their faces. As soon as they rush toward the stairs, I know they must be planning to attack me. I panic and hurry down the street, searching for somewhere to hide. There's a decrepit looking shop just up ahead, the door to which is wide open and half off its hinges. I duck inside and run behind the counter. That's when I realize that my lantern is going to give me away. I can't do anything about it, it's not like I can just make it stop shining. I think about smashing it on the floor, but that will just leave me without a light source.

As I'm trying to hide the lantern in a cabinet, I notice a revolver lying a few feet away. It's so dark I almost didn't see it. I reach for it and check to see if it's loaded. It looks like it's been fired once, but five shots should be enough. There's only two people after me. I peer over the counter. I'm just hoping I've lost my pursuers. It seems like they should've gotten here already. As I stand up, I notice a few extra rounds of ammo lying on the counter top. I snatch them up and place them in my coat pockets.

That's when I see them, out in the street. It's the two men from the balcony. I gasp and try to duck out of sight, but it's too late, they've already seen me. Without thinking, I raise the revolver and fire a single shot at them. One of the men recoils as the bullet rips into his arm. He curses and charges into the shop. Before either of then can get to me, I've already snatched up the lantern and begun to ascend a nearby staircase. I've only used a gun a couple of times before this, and both times I was in the Plains playing Shadow Hunt. Back there, it didn't matter how many times I missed, the gun never ran out of ammo. The cartridges would return to their original state soon after firing them. Here, it's a different story.

I've only got a few shots and who knows whether or not I'll need to use this on anyone else? I'd rather not waste time trying to shoot my pursuers. If I can, I'd prefer to lose them. As I reach the top of the stairs, I bolt into a nearby room and slam the door behind me. Glancing around, I notice a window across the room. As I approach it, I can see that I can get onto the roof from it. I set my lantern on the floor and open the window with my free hand. That's when the door flings open. I snatch up the lantern and fire at the closest of the two. The round strikes him square in the chest and he stumbles backward, knocking his companion to the ground. That's two shots. I scramble out the window and drop onto the slanted roof.

I race to the edge of the roof and stop just short of the ledge. The roof to the next building is too high to jump to. I glance to my left and see that the roof arcs upward. If I can get higher up, I should be able to jump it. I spot the second man climbing out the window and fire at him. The round strikes the glass above him and shatters. He flinches and slows at the sound of the gun, giving me a few extra seconds. Once I get high enough on the roof, I leap to the next building. I land hard and stumble forward, but manage to retain my balance. As I get halfway across the roof, I hear a thud and turn to see that my pursuer has followed and is running straight at me. I panic and bolt across the roof, not daring to stop for even a second. I glance over my shoulder to see that he's beginning to catch up with me as I near the end of the roof. It seems like it might be a much more difficult jump ahead.

As I get closer, I can see that the distance between this building and the next is at least a few feet further than before, and I won't have the advantage of leaping from a greater height. It's either ditch the lantern, or lose the gun. I have to decide quick. At the last possible second, I make the foolish decision to keep hold of both. I leap for the building. The jump is a little too far, and in a panic I toss the lantern onto the roof before I collide with the side of the building. I manage to hang on with my free hand, but I have to toss the gun up on the roof as well. I scramble to pull myself up, but as soon as I do so, my pursuer lands on the roof next to me.

I dive for the gun and he kicks it away. Before I can react, he's picked me up and begun to squeeze me in a bear hug. I struggle to get free, but he just laughs at my efforts. Feeling desperate, I slam the back of my head into his nose, causing him to cry out in pain. He loosens his grasp, but doesn't let go. I make another attempt and kick him in the knee with the heel of my boot. He stumbles and loses his grip, allowing me a brief window of opportunity to escape. I rush for the revolver and snatch it up. As I'm turning to face my attacker, he strikes me across the cheek, sending me reeling. Without intending to, I fire the gun once as I stumble backward. The round sails into the sky and I take aim with my final shot ready to fire. The blast leaves my ears ringing and I watch as he collapses. Wasting no time, I grab my lantern and run as far away as possible. The gunshots have attracted some angry locals. Things aren't looking good. I need to find a place to hide.

Before I leap to the next roof only a few feet away, I take a moment to glance down at the street. Sure enough, I can see at least a dozen or more people swarming about like angry bees. Some are searching the nearby buildings and alleyways. It's only a matter of time until they find me. None of the people seem angry. They seem excited. As I continue to watch, gunshots ring out and people begin brawling in the streets. Screams of rage and agony fill the air. Those caught in the crossfire attempt to flee the area. These people are monsters. They're reveling in the chaos, enjoying every second of it. A familiar voice calls out to me from the nearby rooftop and I see Grenda and Genevieve waving at me.

"Wendy! Come on!" Genevieve hollers, motioning for me to follow. I race for the edge of the roof and leap to the next. As I catch up to them, they begin heading to a nearby fire escape.

"Is it just you two?" I pant, struggling to keep up with them.

"Tom's waiting for us nearby," Genevieve replies, "It's just us four." Once we reach the bottom of the fire escape, I toss the lantern to Grenda who's at the bottom of a rusted ladder. After I've climbed down, Grenda returns my lantern and the four of us head onto an abandoned street.

"This way!" Grenda shouts as she takes the lead. The three of us sprint toward an open man-hole. Grenda stops just short of it. She kneels down and scrambles down a ladder, disappearing from view.

"Go, go, go!" Genevieve orders. She takes my lantern and pushes me toward the hole. As I descend the ladder, a horrid smell fills my nostrils. It's so nauseating that I almost vomit once I reach the bottom.

"Heads up, Wendy!" Genevieve calls to me. She drops the lantern down the hole. I catch it, but it burns my hands and I pass it off to

Grenda. Genevieve comes part way down and heaves the cover back over the hole. She hurries down the ladder and takes the lantern from Grenda. It's at this point that I realize Tom is further down the tunnel, holding his own lantern. Genevieve leads us down the tunnel, further and further into the sewers.

"Just a little further," Genevieve informs us, "We can stop and rest soon."

"What happened back there?" Tom asks me.

"I have no idea," I pant, reloading my revolver while I speak, "I was looking for you and everyone else. While I was doing that, two men came running after me."

"So that was you we heard shooting, wasn't it?" Tom surmises.

"It was at first," I explain, "but just before you all showed up, someone else was shooting. I'm guessing you weren't the only ones who heard the shots. I must have helped stir up the crowd back there. There couldn't have been more than a few minutes between the moment they spotted me and when you all found me."

"It's a good thing you found that revolver," Grenda says as our group comes to a stop, "We might not have found you alive." I raise my pistol and brandish it at Grenda. She gasps and stumbles back into the wall.

"Oh, so I'm your friend now?" I snap, "Why would you be worried about finding me?"

"What do you think you're doing?" Grenda panics.

"You and your idiot sister got us into this mess!" I snarl, "I should put one right between your eyes! It's your fault we're here!"

"Simmer down, Wendy," Genevieve cuts in. She places her hand on my weapon and gently lowers it, "I've already discussed this with her. She says neither of them knew about Linda's intentions and we're going to leave it at that. Right now we need to focus on finding the others."

"I don't believe her," I growl.

"I'm with Wendy on this one," Tom declares. He crosses his arms and glares at Grenda, "She and her sister were both against us from the beginning. How do we know she's telling the truth?"

"You don't," Grenda says, "but I swear I didn't know. I was just doing what Wendy asked of me and took you to Linda. I didn't know she would round us all up and toss us down here. She never mentioned anything of the sort. I've never been loyal to her. She's only controlled

Glenda and I with threats. After this, I won't be going back to her. I've had it. I'll do whatever I can to help from this point on."

"Oh, like that means anything!" I snap, "You said Linda tossed you down here once before already, and you still continued to work for her."

"True, but it was just Glenda and I back then," Grenda replies, "What were we supposed to do? We were outnumbered by her other goons. Things are different this time with you and the others around. You can help us."

"That reminds me," Tom interrupts, "How did you two get her to help you?"

"That's not important," Genevieve answers with a dismissive wave.

"Oh, I think it is," Tom asserts, "Did you make some kind of deal with her? Bribe her? Because beating the snot out of her until she cooperated just wouldn't happen in the Plains, and we all know that."

"I said it's not important!" Genevieve insists.

"No one in the Plains has any need for money," Tom continues, "So I doubt that was the case."

"Shut it, Tom!" Genevieve snarls, "We'll explain everything later; once we've regrouped and escaped this hell hole!" Genevieve glares at him with the light from the lanterns flickering across her face. I look at her, then at Tom, and then at Grenda. For the first time I can see them in color. Their eyes, their hair, their skin, and clothes. As Tom and Genevieve continue arguing, I take a moment to examine all three of them. Grenda's skin is a light brown and her eyes are gray. Her hair is black and her clothes a mix of blue, red, and black.

Tom's eyes are green and his hair is brown with skin much like Grenda's, but a little darker. Genevieve's eyes are an icy blue, her hair is red, and her skin is still rather pale. Tom's clothes are mostly brown and dark green, while Genevieve's are a mix of purple, black, and blue. Back in the world of the living, I never would've cared about such details, but after never seeing any of these three in anything but black and white, it's almost amazing. Grenda sees me staring and clears her throat. I glance at her and then down at my feet.

"You're just now realizing it, aren't you?" she asks, moving closer to me, "Am I the only one who's surprised that Genevieve has red hair?"

"It's just...strange," I reply, "Never thought I'd see a Shadow in anything but black and white."

"Well, anyway," Grenda mumbles, "I guess we should get these two to stop arguing."

"...just would prefer for everyone to stop keeping secrets from me!" Tom snaps.

"We're wasting our time arguing!" Genevieve shouts. Just as she finishes her sentence, Grenda lets out an ear piercing whistle. Genevieve and Tom give irritated groans and turn to face us.

"We've rested long enough," Grenda barks, "Now let's get going. We can't leave until we've found everyone, and I don't know about you two, but I want out of here as soon as possible! The Abyss will swallow us up if we waste too much time." The four of us stand in an intense silence for several moments before someone speaks.

"Let's get moving," Genevieve orders, motioning for us to follow, "Grenda's right. We're getting short on time."

Chapter 15

"What do you mean we're short on time?" I ask.

"The Abyss isn't just a terrible place full of wicked souls," Grenda explains, "It also traps them here for eternity. Even if any Condemned found a way out, they wouldn't be able to leave. Their souls are bound to the Abyss."

"It takes time for a soul to become trapped here," Grenda cuts in, "Just a few brief hours is all it will take, and we've been here for at least an hour as it is."

Our group continues on in silence, navigating the narrow tunnels. After a while I've gotten used to the smell, but I still notice it. At least I'm not feeling nauseated any longer. As I'm pouring over everything I've just heard, I feel a sharp sting of fear. It's so strong that I feel as though I've had the wind knocked out of me. Even so, I continue forward, making certain not to fall behind the others. If this thing about a time limit is true, then we can't afford to slow down for any reason. This isn't the first time I've felt this kind of fear. It's the feeling of being helpless, feeling as though you're standing in the shadow of an approaching tidal wave, and knowing that when it comes crashing down, it's all over. Out of nowhere, memories begin to swirl within my mind. It's as though they're being spun and swirled about by a tornado. Fragments of countless memories appear and vanish as quickly as they come. I stumble and just about lose my balance.

"Are you okay, Wendy?" Grenda asks. The others stop and turn to face me. All at once, I can't take it anymore, I just feel the need to scream...so that's what I do. I scream until I can't anymore. I collapse on the ground and begin shaking as tears stream down my face.

"What's wrong with her?" Grenda panics.

"It's the nature of the Abyss," Genevieve replies, kneeling beside me, "It's forcing her to remember."

"Remember what?" Tom asks. I can see it all. The flames surrounding me, the fear that gripped me. Next I see the bodies of my aunt and uncle lying on the floor. Blood is pooling around them. The police are taking me away, they're telling me that I did it. That I killed them, but I could never remember doing it. Not until now.

"Wendy, what's going on?" Genevieve asks, "What are you seeing?"

I blink and I'm no longer with my friends. I'm lying on the basement floor of my old home. I'm a small child again, bound and gagged. I'm struggling to move, but I can't. Flames are spreading around me and the heat is unbearable. There are pieces of a broken lantern lying a few feet in front of me. With some effort I manage to reach one of the larger pieces of glass. As I'm struggling to cut the ropes, I notice the heavy scent of kerosene in the air. I remember now. I remember why I came to Red Oak. The ropes come loose and I hear someone walking around on the floor above me. My aunt and uncle, my tormentors. They'd left me down there, tied me up so I wouldn't scream or run away. They threw that lantern down here, they wanted the blaze to consume me. As I was trying to free myself, something changed. It was as if I'd enetered a trance. I waited for them by the stairs. They tried to escape, but I wouldn't let them. I stole one of my uncle's revolvers and shot them dead.

My aunt tried to run, but I shot her twice. She fell to the ground and I shot her in the head. I was so enraged that I wanted to make sure she didn't survive. Then I turned to my uncle and did the same. I put the last bullet in his back, straight through his heart. I had to know they were dead. I threw the gun down and watched as the flames spread into the living room. They had planned this. They always said they "never asked to be parents." I was a burden to them. As if it was my fault my parents died. They doused everything in kerosene and tried to leave in the middle of the night. As the smoke begins to fill the house, I calmly walk outside and collapse in the yard. As I'm lying on my back, staring up at the night sky, a familiar voice reaches me ears.

"You're one step closer..." I can tell right away that it's Jessica. I close my eyes for a moment, and when I open them again, I'm my present self. I stare down at my unconscious 9-year-old self. Jessica is standing a few feet from me, her back to the raging inferno that has engulfed my house.

"What is this?" I demand, "Tell me!"

"The Abyss forces souls to relive the most terrible parts of their lives," Jessica answers, "Do you recall what was in your hand when you dreamed of the ruins of Red Oak? What were you holding when that dream began?"

"A bottle," I reply.

"You drank all these memories away," Jessica explains while pieces of my home begin to collapse in the flames.

"What are you talking about? I've never drank in my life!"

"Your mind is repairing itself," Jessica replies, "So long as you remain in the Abyss, these memories will continue to haunt you, just as they haunt Sybil." My eyes widen in shock as Jessica steps aside. Sybil is standing there, motionless. Tears rolling down her cheeks. She falls to her knees beside my younger self.

"I'm sorry, Wendy..." she whispers, "I had to..." Something is wrong. My younger self isn't burned. Her hands and arms are perfectly fine.

"That's...that's not right..." I stutter, staring down at myself, "I...I was burned in the fire! I know it!"

"There is far more to this story than you're seeing," Jessica warns, "Be careful with how you approach this..." Jessica waves her hand and a wall of flames surrounds me. I scream in terror fire as the engulfs me. My eyes snap open and I sit up in a panic.

Chapter 16

It's so dark I can't see. The air is warm and humid. I can feel my heart pounding in my chest. Where am I? A dim light begins to spread around me and I see that I'm in a long corridor. As I drag myself to my feet, the lamps lining the hallway begin to light up, one at a time until the entire corridor is lit up. Looking around, there doesn't seem to be any way out. The gates behind me are sealed shut and it doesn't matter how much I push against them, they won't budge. It seems I have no choice but to move forward. Near the end, I can see an open door.

Before I get even twenty feet, I jump in alarm and turn to see that an iron gate has slammed down from the ceiling. It missed me by only a few inches. The spikes on the ends of the bars are dug into the cobblestone floor. I turn and glance down the hallway, looking for anything that might indicate another gate. After a few moments I start walking again. Three steps...nine steps...seventeen. No gates yet. My breathing is so shallow that I'm getting dizzy. I can't be caught off guard like that again. I don't know if this is a dream, the Abyss, or someplace else. The floor starts to shake and I stumble into a wall. I look over my shoulder to see that the floor is crumbling away. I stumble forward and begin racing down the corridor. Just as I'm certain I'll fall, I leap forward and crash onto a sturdy section of floor. Another gate slams down and nearly impales my arm. As I get to my feet, I can see that I don't have much further to go. I'm more than half way to the end.

I take a deep breath and stare down the corridor. My heart is pounding. What if I don't make it? No...I can't think like that. As I'm watching the doorway, I notice a shadow of a person cast from inside. A flicker of hope runs through me. Maybe they can help me. I start forward again and once more a gate slams behind me. This time it came from the wall. I could feel the wind as it sailed past me. It's in that moment that I begin to panic. I dart forward and two more gates slam behind me. One shoots up from the floor and embeds in the ceiling. The second comes from the wall.

I back away and jump in alarm as another gate closes behind me. My heart sinks when I realize I'm trapped. I take hold of the bars and try in vain to get them to budge. It isn't long before I hear strange screeching sounds coming from beyond the walls. I take another look at the bars and see that I may be able to squeeze through. The sound of insects scuttling in the walls reaches my ears. I glance around for any sign of them, but there's nothing to be seen.

"Hey!" I shout through the bars, "Is someone in there?" No response. "I could use some help here! Hello?" Nothing.

I take a deep breath and put one arm through the bars. My shoulder is a little bigger than the space between, but maybe I can force my way through. More sounds of scuttling prompt me to try harder. Soon I have my torso through the bars, but I'm having trouble getting my legs through. Whatever is moving around in the walls, I don't want to see it. I just want to get out of here. I pull on my leg with all my strength, but if I try much harder, I'll dislocate it. Bit by bit, I manage to squeeze one leg through. I look up to see the ceiling splitting open. A swarm of massive, green insects with sharp pincers begin falling to the floor. One of them latches onto my ankle and I struggle to shake it off. I can feel its pincer getting close to piercing my boot.

"Get off!" I shout. I begin flailing my leg around as much as I can. The insect loses its grasp, but more scramble to attack me. My thigh is halfway through the bars. Just a little further, come on! Come on! That's when I feel a pair of pincers sink into my leg. I let out a yelp and my leg comes free. I crawl away from the gate and kick the insects away with my other foot. They keep trying to attack me as I get to my feet. I stomp on several of them. Green splatters of blood stain the cobblestone around their lifeless bodies. The door is now a short distance away.

The insects behind me begin to let out angry shrieks and soon they're scurrying through the bars. I sprint for the door. Cylindrical columns begin shooting out of the floor, walls, and ceiling. Several insects are caught and smashed against the walls and ceiling. I dive through the doorway and tumble across the floor, just as a column crashes down where I once stood. My back strikes a table leg and I let out a groan. Before I can get to my feet, a pair of hands take hold of my arms and I'm pulled to my feet. There's a woman with long black hair, brown skin, and yellow eyes standing before me. Her hair is styled in dreadlocks, the outermost of which are pulled behind her head and secured in a ponytail, leaving the rest to hang loose.

"Wendy! You're here!" she exclaims, "I thought I'd never see you again!"

"What are you talking about? I've never seen you in my life."

"You don't remember me?"

"No!" I snap, "Of course not! I don't even know where I am!"

"It's me, Valeska," she smiles, "I'm your sister."

"My sister?" This must be who Jessica was referring to.

"That's right," she beams.

Valeska..." I murmur, "Someone mentioned you before."

"Oh? And what did they say?"

"They said you're the ruler of the Ashen Plains," I answer.

"I was," she says, "Not anymore. That was a while ago."

"Look, can you help me find a way out of here?" I ask, poking my head out the door. I can see the entire hallway. It's all in one piece. No bugs, no missing floor sections. Nothing.

"You want to leave already?" Valeska laughs, "Have a seat. I've been waiting to talk with you for some time now." I glare at her and remain by the doorway with my arms crossed. She plops down in one of the chairs at the table and beckons for me to join her. I still don't buy that she's my sister...but she does look a lot like me. Her yellow eyes contrast my brown ones, but the shape is similar. Her cheekbones are more prominent, and her skin is noticably lighter than mine. She's also at least ten years older than me. Other than that, there seems to be a resemblance. Maybe she is my sister.

"Come and sit down, stay a while," she smiles. I exhale my held breath and take a seat at the table. She's likely my only hope of getting out of here. If I'm trapped for now, I might as well talk with her. Maybe she can tell me something useful. I don't trust Jessica just yet, but she did say my sister would make a useful ally.

"So...you're my sister?" I murmur.

"I am," she nods, "Well...half-sister. Same mother, different fathers."

"I wouldn't know," I reply, "I don't remember my parents. They died when I was still very young."

"Not true," Valeska counters, "You've met our mother." I raise an eyebrow and she gets up from her seat.

"How do you know?"

"I may seem isolated here, but I can keep watch on just about everything." She picks up a teapot and pours the contents into a small cup.

"Would you like some?" she offers. I shake my head and she puts the pot back.

"I'm not much of a tea drinker," I explain as she sits back down.

"Understandable," she replies. She blows softly across the top of the cup, "It's not for everyone. So...you look like you want to ask me something."

"Yeah, how do I get out of here?" I mutter.

"In time, my dear," she assures me, "Just be patient. I know you have other things weighing on your conscience. It's written all over your face. Why don't you share what you have to say with me? Hmm?"

"If I've met my mother, then who is she?"

"That doesn't seem like something you've been itching to ask," Valeska replies.

"That's because I don't care about her!" I snap, thumping my fists on the table, "She abandoned me and left me with two awful people who made my life Hell! Whoever she is, she can rot in the Abyss for all I care. Along with the aunt and uncle she left me with." She averts her gaze and takes a drink of her tea.

"I can't say I want anything to do with her either," Valeska sighs, "Especially since she tried to kill me...and you." My thoughts go back to the dream I had at the orphanage. I can still hear Annie. 'Don't listen to her! She did this to us!'

"Who was she?" I demand, "Tell me!"

"No need to shout," Valeska grumbles, "I can hear just fine. To answer your question, her name is Maris."

"I've never met a Maris," I reply, "Look, I need to get back to my friends. I can't sit here and waste time."

"Come to think of it, why are you down here anyway?"

"Some woman named Linda threw me and my friends down here," I explain, "What does it-"

"Wait," Valeska interrupts, "Did you say Linda?"

"Yes, that's right."

"Martinez?"

"I believe so," I reply.

"That little wretch!" Valeska rages. She thumps her fist down on the table and stands up with enough force to knock her chair over, "I'll see to it that she spends the rest of eternity in the Witherlands for this!"

"What's wrong?" I ask. I have to force the words out of me. She's got me on edge and I'm almost afraid to stay in the room with her. She takes notice and takes a deep breath before standing her chair back up and sitting down.

"I'm sorry," she grumbles, "It's just...I told her to leave you out of this..."

"You did what?" I snap, "You're the one giving her orders?"

"It's not what you think," Valeska assures me, "Linda was supposed to bring you to me, not toss you into the Abyss. I had a feeling she might betray me."

"You'd better start explaining," I snarl.

"It's as I said before, Wendy," she begins, "Maris, our mother, tried to kill you. When that failed, she took up a renewed interest in you. Surviving your own murder gave her hope that maybe you were stronger than she thought. Our mother is a strange woman...cold...wicked...manipulative. She thinks she can do whatever she wants, but nothing is further from the truth Wendy. You and I were born with a special purpose that no one else can fill. Whoever told you about me was right. I was the ruler of the Plains, I was their Queen...until Maris struck me down."

"And who is Maris?" I ask, "Besides our mother?"

"She is the one who created the four realms," Valeska explains, "The living world, the Abyss, the Plains, and the Oasis. As her children, we were tasked with the responsibility of keeping watch over the three afterlife realms. Instead she betrayed us. Replaced us with the souls of ordinary people. That's how Queen Lydia came to rule the Abyss. She was a wicked, horrible woman in life, and Maris felt she was a perfect candidate to hold the title of Queen of the Damned. The same thing happened with the Oasis and its ruler, Carmen. Naturally I was furious. I felt it wrong for anyone other than Maris's own blood to keep watch over these worlds."

"If she's some kind of deity, as you claim," I begin, "Then how could I have survived? How could someone like her have trouble killing me?"

"The blood we share with Maris makes things complicated," Valeska replies, "We're her equals. She can't just reap our souls like normal humans. However, you were and still are vulnerable. You can be killed the same way as any normal person. That's why she went after you the way she did."

"Is my relation to her why I can travel between worlds?"

"Precisely," Valeska confirms, taking another drink of her tea, "No one except you, me, and Maris can do that."

"What about Annie? How can she come here? She's not my sister too is she?" Valeska closes her eyes and shakes her head.

"It's only us two," she answers, "I would know if there were any others. My guess is that you unknowingly bestowed some of your abilities on her. I used to do the same with some of my friends when I was younger. It's not permanent, and you can take it away from her at any time. Not that I think you need to."

"I should hope not, seeing as you've never even met her."

"True," Valeska smiles, "but like I said, I've been keeping an eye on you and your friends for some time now. It's a...perk...of being Maris's descendant. I could teach you to do it too if you'd like."

"Just slow down for a second. First I want to know why you've been spying on me. Assuming you're telling me the truth, that is."

"Annie passed out when she first saw Sybil," Valeska recounts, "You visited a girl named Claire in the art museum, and you've been having dreams about a train that you don't understand."

"H-How did...?" I stutter, "O-Okay, fine those things happened; but how do you know about that and not what Linda did to me? How she threw me down here?"

"I don't maintain constant watch," she answers, "I can only watch one area at a time. I've been keeping an eye on our traitorous mother as well."

"You still haven't given me a straight answer about her," I growl, "You say I've met her, but I don't remember a Maris. How about telling me what she looks like?"

"She's been walking about under an assumed name," Valeska explains, placing her elbows on the table, "I believe she's calling herself Jessica." Nothing is making any sense to me. Jessica said that Valeska would be an ally. She seems friendly enough, but something isn't right about her. Why would Jessica tell me about her? Clearly Valeska bears a grudge against her.

"I need to go..." I mumble. I stand up from the table and Valeska grabs my arm.

"There's one thing I need to say before you leave," she says. She lets go and stands up, "One of your friends has picked up something important to me. I need you to see to it that it makes it out of the Abyss with you."

"What is it?"

"Our mother locked me away in the Abyss the day she made an attempt on your life," she explains, "My physical form was severely diminished. You're going to need my help if you want to survive. Our mother is still watching you. She's waiting for the moment you piece your forgotten memories back together. She's gotten soft in recent years. You are still her child after all. She wants you to live...but she doesn't want you to remember. Your memory will return very soon. When that happens, she'll find and kill you."

"And why would she do that?"

"Because you and I are a threat to her," Valeska answers, "As long as your memory remains in shambles, she considers you weak. It will take time for you to recover even after you get everything back. That's why I need you to free me."

"How do I know I can trust you?"

"You don't," she replies, "However, if I'm free I can protect you. I know it's difficult since you still can't remember me, but you have to trust me." I glare at her for a few seconds before walking away. I stop at the door. Part of me wants to ignore her and keep walking, but I also feel like I should help her. If what she said is true, then I really can't trust Jessica.

"Fine..." I mutter, "What do I need to do?"

"This place you see before you is an illusion within my own mind, Wendy," she replies, "You will have to find me. As I said, someone else already has. Someone you know."

"I don't understand."

"As I said before, my physical form is diminished," she explains, "I'm afraid that I'm nothing more than a parasite. You'll understand when you find your friend." She claps her hands and I'm back with

Genevieve and the others. I'm lying on my back, looking up at the sky. I sit up in a daze. Did I imagine all of it?It takes me a few moments to realize that we aren't in the sewer anymore. Genevieve is kneeling next to me with her back turned while she helps the others out of the sewer. Tom spots me as he comes up the ladder.

"She's awake," he informs Genevieve. She turns and looks at me with concern.

"Are you alright, Wendy?" Genevieve asks.

"I'm fine," I lie, "I just...I don't know what happened."

Chapter 17

"It happened to Grenda too," Genevieve murmurs. She gestures toward Grenda who's lying unconscious several feet away, "She started screaming about needles and spiders, then she passed out like you."

"I want to get out of here," I mumble, "I'm starting to wonder if I'm losing my mind."

"I know I shouldn't be asking this," Tom grunts as he and Genevieve help me to my feet, "but what did you see?"

"Something I had forgotten," I reply, glancing toward Grenda, "Something I wish I'd never remembered."

Ever since I came to Red Oak, I would have nightmares at least once a month. It was always the same. I was tied up in a basement while flames danced around me, but the dream never went much further than that. I would always wake up screaming and drenched in sweat. This is what Melissa mentioned back at the orphanage before she moved out. How she was irritated that I would wake her up with my shouting.

It was one of the reasons I was sent to see a specialist during my time there. Nothing ever came of it. They tried to hypnotize me, get me to relive the memories I had blocked out. They told me it was for my own good. They said the nightmares would go away if I could figure out what my subconscious was hiding from me. I tried to adapt, to learn to live with my condition. To get used to the fact that I would have nightmares every so often. There had always been a small gap of time missing around the time I came to Red Oak. I assumed I'd buried the memories for a good reason.

"It's a side effect of being in the Abyss," Genevieve explains, "This place will force anyone who either lives or journeys here to relive painful things they endured. What's worse, is it can drive a person to madness."

"Did you have to tell her that?" Tom mutters while he searches for signs of Condemned.

"It would be foolish to ignore the truth about this place," Genevieve counters.

"I suppose," Tom shrugs, "Just seems like a morbid topic is all. We're already on edge as it is and people are still missing. Increasing that tension doesn't seem like a good idea."

"Let's get Grenda up so we can get going," I cut in, "No telling how much longer we'll be safe here."

"Or how much time we have left," Tom adds. As Genevieve and I rouse Grenda from her slumber, an angry shriek cuts through the air. It's faint, but it's close by. We all wait in silence as two more shrieks echo down the deserted streets.

"That's Claire's voice," Tom gasps, racing toward the screams, "Come on! We need to find her!"

"Go with Tom," Genevieve orders as she drags Grenda to her feet, "We'll catch up with you." I nod and hurry after Tom. For a moment, I lose sight of him. Another scream cuts through the air and Tom rushes past me from a nearby alley.

"This way!" he shouts.

"Why were you down there?" I ask, following after him.

"I got turned around, just forget it," Tom replies. We round a corner and stop in our tracks. Claire is standing in the middle of the street, an ax in her hand and her head bowed. She's panting and covered in blood.

"Oh my God..." Tom gasps. On the ground are the mutilated bodies of a middle-aged man and woman. Each of them lie face down in a pool of blood. Nearby I notice Sybil sitting on the front porch of one of the houses. She seems rather calm in spite of what's taking place in front of her. In fact, she's smiling. She looks just like she did when she changed her appearance to avoid scaring Annie. Her hair remains black and her eyes an emerald green. Her skin is fair and her clothes, being a mixture of black and white, don't appear much different from her typical appearance.

"Claire?" Tom calls out as he approaches her. Sybil turns her head and stands up once she spots us.

"Stay back!" Claire snaps. Tom freezes and Sybil steps off the porch. Claire brushes her bangs away from her eyes, part of her face still concealed in shadow.

"What's going on here?" I ask Sybil as she sneaks to my side.

"The Benson's..." Sybil whispers.

"Who?"

"Claire and Tom's parents." Tom takes a few steps closer to his sister and stops when she raises the ax onto her shoulder. She turns her head and glares at Tom.

"I told you to stay back!" she snarls.

"Look, I just want to talk," Tom assures her.

"Well, I don't," Claire growls. I've never seen this side of Claire before. I never knew she was capable of murder. Sure, she seemed a little abrasive at times, but this?

"Claire, we're on a time limit, we need to hurry and find the others," Tom explains, "Please put the ax down. You don't have to say a word. Just come with us so we can get out of here." Claire tosses the ax aside without breaking eye contact.

"It was poison, Tom," she murmurs, "You were right. Isn't that just fantastic? You were right all along, you pessimistic jackass!"

"What are you talking about?" Tom moans, "Right about what?"

"You said it the moment we met up in the Plains," Claire continues, approaching Tom as she speaks, "You said, 'They never much liked us. My money is on poison.' Remember? When I was freaking out? I had just woken up dead and you were already having a damn pity party while I twisted in the wind! You happy now?"

"I still don't understand."

"I'm just telling you that you won, Tom!" Claire bellows, throwing her arms into the air and causing Tom to nearly fumble his lantern, "I kept saying that maybe it was an accident, perhaps we were murdered. Well, I suppose we were murdered, now weren't we? I just never imagined our own parents would be at fault! You want to know what's ironic about this?" she continues, pointing to the two bodies behind her, "That creepy housekeeper they hired after we perished, she used that same poison to kill our parents, take over the estate, and steal our money and possessions! That's why they're here! Isn't that hilarious? She sold my paintings! Damn good thing I hid a few of them! How am I supposed to find the others?"

"Claire, please just calm down-" Tom pleads.

"Calm down?" Claire interrupts, "Calm down? Is that the best you've got? That seems to be the only thing anyone has to say to me. First Sybil tells me to calm down and now you!"

"I don't know what you want me to do!" Tom shouts, hurling his hat to the ground.

"When we get out of here, you're going to help me track down and steal back my paintings!" Claire hisses, "You got that? Every single one of them!"

"Fine, whatever you say!" Tom growls. He scoops his hat off the ground and places it back on his head, "Now can we please get going?"

"What's going on here?" Genevieve shouts from behind me. Everyone stops and turns to face her. With the light of her lantern flickering across her face, I'm reminded of how intimidating she can be.

"We're getting ready to find the others," Sybil responds. Grenda is walking on her own again and standing a few feet behind Genevieve. She looks tired, but otherwise fine.

"That's odd, because it sounded to me like you were wasting time arguing," Genevieve snarks, "Where are Annie and Glenda?"

"We got separated somewhere nearby," Sybil explains, "We stayed in one place in the hopes that they would catch up to us. It couldn't have been more than a few blocks."

"What was all the screaming about?" Genevieve asks.

"I was upset about something..." Claire mumbles, "Forget it, it's not important."

"You sure calm down quick," Tom mutters.

"Shut it, Tom!" Claire snaps.

"Waiting for them to come back, huh?" Genevieve says, glancing at each of us, "Smart decision. Last thing we need is more people getting lost. At least we found you two. Were these Condemned giving you trouble?"

"You could say that," Sybil replies.

"I said it's not important," Claire insists, staring at the ground, "I don't want to hear anything about those two anymore." She steps into a patch of light from a streetlamp and it's the first time I can see her face. Her hair is a deep brown, her eyes are the same color, and her skin is similar to Tom's. Her cheeks and forehead are drenched in sweat and blood is spattered on her hands, face, and clothes. Soon after, I see one of the bodies begin to stir. The man drags himself to his knees and groans. Claire takes notice and turns to face him.

"You should've stayed on the ground old man!" Claire thunders, snatching up the ax and racing toward him. Before he can react, Claire slams the back of the blade into his face. There's a sickening crack and everyone except Genevieve and Sybil cringes. Genevieve smirks and Sybil laughs.

"I love this side of her!" Sybil cackles, "Hit him again!" Claire ignores Sybil's shouts and buries the blade in the man's back. He lets out a cry of agony and collapses on the ground. I grab Sybil by the arm and drag her off to the side. Once we're out of earshot I turn and glare at her.

"What the hell is wrong with you?" I snarl, "She's hacking her own father up with an ax!"

"Oh relax, Wendy," Sybil chuckles, "They're Condemned. Spirits of the Black Abyss. They just revive whenever they get killed." As soon as she says it, I feel stupid for bringing it up. I should've figured there was a reason for why Sybil was so calm. I take a deep breath and stare up at the sky.

"Wendy?" Sybil asks, "Are you...alright?"

"Sybil," I growl, "I want to know something. I want you to tell me the truth."

"What is it?"

"What do you know about the night my aunt and uncle died?"

"Nothing, why?"

"You're lying!" I shout, "I know what you did!" Sybil's eyes narrow and Genevieve and the others all stop and look in our direction.

"So...you remembered..." Sybil mumbles, "You're piecing it all together, aren't you? Wendy, I'm sorry for what I did, but I-"

"I don't want your half-baked apology!" I hiss, slamming her against a wall, "I know it was you who killed my aunt and uncle and I know you possessed me to do it!"

"Wendy, you don't understand!" Sybil snarls, "I did what was necessary for your survival!" I grab her by the front of her dress and smash her into the wall a second time.

"Why did you have to possess me?" I growl, "Why didn't you possess one of them? Make it look like a murder-suicide? Do you have any idea how much that tore me up?"

"It doesn't work that way!" Sybil shouts.

"Then how does it work, Sybil?" I rage, "How the hell does it work?" There's a tense silence. I grit my teeth and glare at the others, then back at Sybil.

"Do you have any idea what this is like?" I growl, "What I'm going through? It's like part of my life is missing! I woke up a few days ago and never questioned anything. I don't even know what's real anymore! Who's lying and who's telling the truth?"

"I've always told you the truth," Sybil insists.

"I know when you're lying, Sybil!" I snarl, "I've known you long enough! I can see it in your eyes!"

"This isn't the place to discuss this," Sybil hisses, "You're vulnerable right now. That's why I'm here with you."

"There's that word again!" I snap, "Vulnerable. How am I vulnerable?"

"It's a long story, Wendy," Sybil replies, "I'm not in any position to tell you, so just drop it!"

"That's why you're here with me?" I repeat, "What are you talking about? What else are you hiding?"

"I didn't meet you by coincidence," Sybil explains, "This is so frustrating. I told her this was a terrible idea, but no. She wouldn't have any of it!"

"Sybil!" Genevieve cuts in, "You need to stop!"

"Piss off!" Sybil snaps, "Things aren't progressing fast enough! We all know what's going on! Everyone except her and she's the one who needs that information the most!"

"That's not your call to make!" Tom fires back. Sybil grabs me by the arm and begins leading me away. The others try to follow and she pulls her knife.

"Stay back!" she shouts, "All of you! I'll slice you to ribbons!" A tense standoff ensues. Everyone but Grenda is glaring at Sybil. Sybil's knife is quivering in her hand. I can't tell if it's from fear, anger, or both.

"You don't make the rules, Sybil!" Claire shouts, "You don't decide what's best!"

"My job is to protect her," Sybil growls, "Don't interfere!"

"This isn't just about you!" Tom cuts in, "This affects us all!"

"I don't care what happens to me!" Sybil shrieks, "As long as she's safe, it doesn't matter!"

"You could be putting her in danger with anything you say to her," Genevieve warns.

"We're not against you, Sybil," Claire adds, "but don't think you're the only one who's concerned for Wendy! We all want this to go right, not just you!"

"I am her Sentinel!" Sybil rages, "I've been with her since the beginning! You don't know what my job is like! You will never understand! I saved her from the fire! I guard her life! You idiots just happened along years after I was assigned to her! Do you have any idea of the burden I carry every single day? Back off and let me do my job!" Just as Sybil's through speaking, I raise my revolver and fire a single round into the air. Everyone jumps in alarm.

"Wendy?" Sybil whispers. I glare at her and she lets go of my arm. She backs away as I replace the spent cartridge.

"You've got a lot of explaining to do," I hiss, "What the hell was all that? Sentinel? Assigned to me? Your job? What the hell are you talking about?"

"I lost my temper, Wendy," Sybil mutters, staring at the ground while she speaks, "I've said too much already..."

"How do you expect me to trust you?" I rage, "Now I know you've been keeping secrets from me!"

"They aren't secrets if you already know them," Sybil mumbles.

"But I don't!" I shout, "How can you even say that?"

"Because it's true!" Sybil snaps, "This is why I didn't say anything! I wanted you to be safe! To be happy! I knew you would remember on your own. Telling you all at once would have been a shock." She looks back up at me with a look of frustration. Her grip on her knife is so tight that her knuckles are turning white.

"Before we discuss anything else, I want to know about the fire."

"You already know what happened," Sybil mutters, "What else can I tell you?"

"Why did you use me to kill them?" I demand, "Tell me!"

"I had to..." Sybil whispers, "It's like I said. I was assigned to protect you, I couldn't let you die. That was unacceptable. She would've had my head if it were possible."

"Careful, Sybil..." Genevieve warns.

"What aren't you telling me?" I ask Genevieve, "Is Jessica controlling the lot of you? That's who she's talking about, right?"

"It's not like that, I give you my word," Sybil assures me, "I would never willfully keep a secret from you, Wendy. You must know that by now."

"Look," Genevieve begins, brushing her hair behind her ear, "Plain and simple, you lost part of your memory. We have to allow you to remember on your own, but Sybil is frustrated because we don't have the luxury of time. You're in danger and we don't know how to speed this process up in a safe way."

"Then spit it out!" I rage, shoving Genevieve backward. She stumbles a few paces and regains her balance, a look of sorrow in her eyes.

"I'm sorry, Wendy," Genevieve murmurs, "I can't imagine what it must be like in your shoes, but we have other things to worry about right now. I know you don't want to, but it would be best if we dropped this for now."

"Anyone else want to tell me what they know?" I demand. As I glance around, I see Claire place the ax over her shoulder and look away. Tom grips his lantern and places his free hand in his coat pocket. He stares down at the ground and clears his throat.

"Don't look at me," Grenda shrugs, "I just met you people." Sybil places her hand on my shoulder.

"We're on your side," Sybil assures me, "Genevieve is right. We need to focus our attention on the task at hand. We need to find Annie and Glenda. We'll discuss this later, I promise." As angry as I am in this moment, I know she's right. None of this will matter if we all become trapped in the Abyss.

Sybil motions for everyone to follow her. I don't know how much more of this I can take. My world is falling down around me.

Chapter 18

Minutes tick by as I continue down the street, lost in thought at the back of the group. Sybil keeps turning her head to check on me every so often, but no one speaks to me. At this point, I could care less about what they have to say. Right now I feel like Grenda is the only one I can trust. She's the only one who doesn't seem to know what's happening. Even if that's true, and she really is out of the loop, I still haven't known her for more than a few hours. I could care less if she claims that she's no longer loyal to Linda. It doesn't mean anything. Those are just words.

"Anyone else find it strange that we haven't been attacked since finding Wendy?" Claire inquires while we make our way through the crowd.

"Not all Condemned are hostile," Genevieve explains, "A lot of them are passive, too wrapped up in their own thoughts to care about anything else."

"Any chance we could ask them if they've seen the others?" Tom suggests. We round a corner and head down a street filled with dilapidated houses.

"It would be a waste of time," Genevieve replies with a wave of her hand, "Like I said, they're too wrapped up in themselves to care." Continuing down the street, I watch the people around us. Some are huddled together along the front of buildings, one is rocking back and forth near an alley, and many others are wandering the streets. All of them have somber or pained expressions.

"I can't imagine spending eternity in a place like this," Grenda shudders, "They all look so...anguished."

"They should," Genevieve says, "They aren't capable of feeling things like love and joy. Hate, fear, jealousy, sorrow, anger, it never ends for them. The worst part is that they still remember what it was like before this."

"And it just goes on forever?" Tom asks, "The Abyss, that is."

"I believe so," Genevieve answers.

"I see..." Tom murmurs.

"I'm not sure about this," Genevieve begins, "but I've heard that Lydia's servants wander around this place, keeping an eye on the Condemned. You'd never be able to tell them apart in appearance. They do seem a little more sane than the others. At least the ones I've met." As I'm listening, I think back to that woman who gave me the lantern. Reika. Could she have been one of Lydia's servants?

"Along with that, they all came here the same way, all committed evil acts in life," Genevieve continues, "What I've heard is that every so often, they find and abduct Condemned, then take them back to Lydia who decides what to do with them."

"So, then what?" Claire asks.

"She decides whether or not their souls are pure enough to send to the Plains," Genevieve answers, "They can never go to the Oasis, but the Plains is still an improvement over this place." A shrill scream pierces the air. Up ahead of us, I can see a disturbance in the crowd. Three gunshots ring out and I hear the woman scream a second time. It takes me a moment, but I soon realize it sounds familiar.

"That's Annie!" I shout, bolting past the others. Soon Annie comes into view. Her face is drained of color and her eyes wild with panic. She spots me and begins racing in my direction. The crowd scatters as three pursuers come into view behind her. I draw my revolver and fire. The first round misses and strikes a lamppost. The second and third hit the female pursuer in the arm and chest. She crashes to the ground and drops her crowbar. Annie rushes behind me, the crowd dissolving into chaos around us. Sybil races past me and knocks me off balance. She tackles one of Annie's attackers and sinks her knife into his neck. The third attacker kicks Sybil to the ground and raises a steel pipe over his head. In a panic, I fire my last three rounds.

One strikes the man in the arm and another hits his ribs. He stumbles and turns to face me and Annie. He charges at us and knocks us to the ground. He swings his pipe at me, missing by inches as I roll to avoid it. I hear Claire let out a shrill, angry cry and look up to see that she's lodged her ax in the man's back. He falls to the ground and Claire strikes him multiple times, splattering blood all over the street. A gunshot echoes from a nearby doorway. Claire screams and flees for cover as two more shots are heard. I just barely catch a glimpse of Tom wrestling the gun away from the shooter as multiple Condemned race by me. I hear another gunshot as I get to my feet. Tom hurls the shooter to the ground and finishes the man off with a shot to the forehead. He then runs to me and Annie with a rifle in one hand and his lantern in the other.

"Come on!" he shouts over the screams, "We need to find the others." He passes his lantern to Annie and I spot Sybil heading into an alley. I motion for the others to follow her.

"Wendy!" Genevieve shouts from behind us. We turn to see both her and Grenda heading toward us.

"What's going on?" Genevieve hollers over the noise, "Where are the others?"

"I saw Sybil heading this direction," I reply, "Her and Claire are this way." We push through the crowd and into the alley where we find Sybil tending to Claire.

"What happened?" Tom panics. Sybil is in the middle of bandaging Claire's leg with strips of her own clothing. Both of them are covered in blood. Just how much is Claire's is impossible to tell.

"Someone shot me!" Claire snarls, attempting to stand, "What do you think happened?" She yelps and falls back into a seated position.

"Stay put and let me finish!" Sybil snaps.

"Who?" asks Genevieve, glancing at me and Tom.

"Not them, you idiot," Claire groans, "It was that guy in the doorway. The one Tom killed."

"Couldn't shoot anyone if I wanted to now," I mutter, tossing the empty gun on a nearby crate, "I'm out of ammo."

"Hang on to it anyway," Genevieve orders. She swipes it up and hands it back to me, "We may find more ammo. Better to have it just in case. We need to hurry and find the last missing member of our group. The sooner we get Claire to the Plains, the sooner that wound will heal."

"She can't even walk," Sybil points out, finishing with the bandaging, "How are we supposed to get anywhere? We're low on time as it is and we can't just drag her along. We'll never get out of here."

"Glad to know I've doomed us all," Claire mutters.

"Just stand her up for a second," Tom instructs, "I'll carry her for now, but I'm going to need someone to switch with at some point."

"Good idea," Genevieve grunts, helping Sybil lift Claire to her feet. Claire grits her teeth as they help her onto Tom's back. Once they're both sure she won't fall, we leave the alley and turn onto another street.

"How far are we from the gate?" Sybil asks.

"We've been heading east, so I know we're heading in the right direction," Genevieve replies, "As for how far, I'd estimate maybe two miles. I won't know for sure until I get a good look around. There should be a clock tower in this area. The faces are all mixed up, each showing different times. One of them says 3:27."

"And what does that mean?" Sybil asks.

"There's a tavern two buildings over from that side of the tower," Genevieve explains, "Beneath it is a system of tunnels that lead to a gate that connects to the Plains."

"Won't we need a key to use it?" Grenda asks.

"I've already covered that," Genevieve assures us, "We just need to find that tavern."

"We need to find Glenda first," Sybil says.

"Yeah, then get back in time to help Franklin," Tom adds, "If all went according to plan, he's found Adrienne by now I just hope the two of them can handle things until we get back."

"They'll be fine," Genevieve assures him, "There's nothing to worry about, assuming he got to Adrienne in time. They should be able to buy us more than enough time, even if it's just the two of them."

"Glenda should be somewhere down here," Annie says, pointing down the empty street, "We took refuge in a hospital down this way."

"Let's hurry and find her," Tom grunts as Claire shifts her weight, "Once we're out, we'll need to deal with Linda." With all that's been happening here in the Abyss, I had almost forgotten about Linda. There's no telling what sort of damage she might do if we don't get to her soon. I just hope Adrienne can do something to stop her, or at the very least slow her down. As we move down the street, I catch glimpses of Condemned wandering the area. Some are crying, others staring into the sky. I watch as two Condemned work to cut down a third hanging from a noose. They cut through the rope and he tumbles to the street below. I gasp as the scene unfolds before me. He lands with a sickening crack, splattering blood on the pavement. I wonder if he hanged himself so he would stay unconscious? So he wouldn't have to face the reality of being trapped in this place. A bottle whizzes past Sybil's head and shatters on the street. The entire group turns to see a haggard woman sitting on a second story windowsill. She laughs and watches us walk by.

"Damn hag," Sybil mutters, "Too bad killing her wouldn't do anything."

"Don't let them get to you," Claire says, "They're trapped here and we're not." Off to my right, I hear my name being called. The entire group comes to a halt and I spot Reika standing nearby.

"Wendy!" she calls out. She waves and beckons for me to come see her.

"Who's that?" Clare asks.

"Nobody," I mutter, locking eyes with Reika.

"A nobody who knows your name?" Claire snorts. I shake my head in frustration and walk over to Reika. She's holding a small pouch in her left hand.

"You're still alive," Reika observes, "She'll be happy to hear that."

"Who will?"

"No one," Reika replies with a wave of her hand, "Here...take this and go." She hands me the pouch and begins to walk away. Before she can, I grab her arm and pull her back.

"I know it's Jessica," I snarl, "Do me a favor and tell her I'm on to her. I want to speak with her as soon as possible."

"I'll let her know," Reika says with a wink. She walks off and disappears into the crowd. I look down at the pouch in my hand and walk back to the group.

"What was that all about?" Sybil asks.

"Don't worry about it," I mutter while we continue down the street. I open the pouch to find a about three dozen pistol cartridges. I place one in my revolver and see that it matches the empty casings still inside. How did she know? Once I'm finished reloading my weapon, I pocket the pouch and continue on. Who is that woman? I suspect that Jessica might be ordering her around, but even that doesn't make much sense. I barely know Jessica.

I gasp as a man crashes through a window and lands in the street. Sinister cackles can be heard inside the building. A mug sails through another window and soon I hear tables and chairs being overturned.

The others and I all continue down the street, bracing for an attack that never comes. Grenda drops to the back of the group and walks beside me. She grabs my arm and forces me to slow down for a moment, dropping us just out of earshot of the others.

"I wanted to ask you something," Grenda murmurs, "About that woman. The one you just spoke to a little while ago."

"What about her?"

"Who is she?"

"I don't know."

"What rubbish!" Grenda snaps. Sybil and Genevieve both glance over their shoulders at us for a moment.

"Her name is Reika, that's all I know," I grumble, "I don't know who she is, I don't know why she's helping me. She gave me a lantern before this. That's it. I don't know anything else."

"Look, I don't know what they're hiding from you, Wendy, but I do know this," Grenda continues, "I'm almost certain that I've seen that Reika woman around here before. Condemned never take up an interest in visitors like us. Not unless someone ordered them to."

"I don't know anything else," I repeat.

"Stop bothering her," Sybil snaps as she approaches us. The others stop and stare.

"She's not bothering me," I lie.

"She is if I say she is," Sybil mutters. She grabs Grenda's arm and begins to lead her to the front of the group.

"Lay off, Sybil," I growl. She sighs and lets go of Grenda's arm, "Grenda can speak to me all she wants. It's not a problem."

"It is a problem," Sybil snarls, "There are bigger things at work here, Wendy. Things you know nothing about."

"That has nothing to do with Grenda!" I hiss. Claire and Tom look back at me with looks of sympathy.

"Fine, whatever," Sybil mutters. As she's walking away, I see we've arrived at the hospital Annie mentioned earlier.

"Where did you see her last?" Genevieve asks Annie.

"We were on the bottom floor," Annie answers, "We hid near the morgue. I could probably find the room, but I can't guarantee anything. When we got separated I ran through the halls in a panic with those Condemned after me. It's all one big blur." Sybil jogs up the front steps and reaches for the door. Just as she takes hold of the handle, the door crashes open and two men race out of the building in a panic. Sybil tumbles down the stairs and lands in a heap. She jumps to her feet and draws her knife. Genevieve grabs her by the wrist before she can take off after the two Condemned.

"Let go of me!" Sybil snarls.

"It's not worth wasting anymore time," Genevieve argues. Sybil lowers the knife and I can see that she's bleeding from her hand and cheek. She shakes Genevieve loose and heads into the building. As the rest of us follow after Sybil, Annie takes the lead. Genevieve begins directing everyone to change positions. Annie, with her lantern, pairs with Sybil at the front. Grenda takes Genevieve's lantern and falls to the back of the group. Tom hands over his rifle to Genevieve and she motions for me to guard Tom and Claire from their left side while she takes the right.

With the exception of some occasional thumps and creaks, the building is silent for now, but there's no telling how long that will last. Somewhere in the building I can hear footsteps, doors opening and slamming, various thumping noises. Annie motions for us to follow her down an adjacent hallway. At the end of it, I can see that part of the ceiling has collapsed. Annie mentions it as a landmark and stands staring at it for a moment before she turns right. I don't pay much attention to her conversation with Sybil, but I do hear that she's having trouble remembering where to go.

Understandable since she fled in a panic. Angry shouts echo from the floor above. Dust and rubble sprinkle down upon us. We all wait for the footsteps above us to fade. As I'm exhaling my held breath, Annie whispers for us to follow her. She says we're near the morgue. Glenda should be close by. I can tell Grenda is eager to find her sister. She starts to move to the front of the group, but stops herself and re-takes her position. Tom seems to be getting tired. He's been carrying Claire since she was shot. He hasn't asked anyone to take a turn carrying her yet. For a moment, I consider giving it a shot, but Claire is taller than me. I'm not sure I'd be able to carry her very far. Not only that, I need my hands free to use my revolver. Though, I could just pass it to someone else. Maybe there's another way I can help. I start peeking into the nearby rooms.

"Wendy?" Claire asks, "What's going on? What are you looking for?"

"A wheelchair," I reply, "There has to be one around here somewhere."

"Good idea," Tom grunts. As I enter the next room, I can just make out a mangled bed and debris all over the floor. I'm mostly going by feel since I can't see anything without my lantern. Luckily the rooms aren't all that big. As I'm coming back out, I catch my foot on something covered with a sheet and I fall to the ground with a thud. The sheet falls on top of me and Sybil pulls it off.

"There we go," I grunt as Sybil helps me up.

"Good thinking, Wendy," Sybil says, spotting the wheelchair. We move it out of the room and into the hall. It's only there for a moment, but I see a flicker of relief on Tom's face as Claire slides off his back and hobbles toward the chair. Sybil and I seat her in it and Tom begins pushing her down the hall.

"I just had a thought," Claire says, "There were steps at the front of this building and I imagine there will be other places where using this would be difficult."

"We'll cross that bridge when we come to it," Tom assures her.

"I think the room is just down here," Annie says, pointing to a room across from the morgue. Grenda breaks away from the group and darts toward the room. She stops at the door and begins trying to push it open. Annie rushes to help, but the door won't budge.

"She must have barricaded herself inside," Annie grunts, giving the door another push.

"Well, come on then!" Grenda urges with a frantic wave, "Help us push!"

Genevieve and I join in and inch by inch the door opens. A loud crash echoes from the other side and Grenda worms her way inside.

"Better get ready," Genevieve warns the rest of us, "No telling who might have heard that just now." I hear Grenda let out a muffled scream and return to the door. She has one hand over her mouth and tears forming in her eyes. With her free arm, she gestures for me to follow her inside. After I squeeze inside, I see that a lamp is filling the room with a dim light. In the corner is Glenda. Her back is turned to us and she has her knees pulled up to her chest, rocking back and forth. Her arms appear to have large needles stabbed straight through them. Blood covers her arms and hands and has stained her clothes.

"What happened to her?" I ask as Grenda tries to get her sister to turn around.

"I don't know," Grenda quavers, "Glenda! Glenda, come on! We're going home!" Glenda pushes her sister back and gets to her feet. She remains facing the wall.

"Wendy, hurry and ask someone to find some bandages," Grenda implores. I nod and head back to the door. I poke my head out and repeat Grenda's request. Tom asks why, but I shake my head and withdraw back into the room. I don't know if Grenda wants the others to know what's going on. As I close the door, I hear Glenda speak for the first time since I last saw her.

"I can't..." she whispers, "I have to stay. I have to. It's where I belong."

"Rubbish!" Grenda snaps. She carefully removes one of the needles and discards it, "You belong with me, back in the Plains." Grenda removes another needle and tosses it aside. I can tell she's trying to avoid opening a damaged artery. She stops as she draws out a third needle.

"This isn't going to work," Grenda groans, "I could end up making her bleed to death. We need to do something about them, though. We can't have them getting caught on anything."

"Can we break them?" I ask.

"Like snap them apart? No, I don't think so. It'll take too long and I might hurt her even more trying to bend them. Check the drawers for something, anything. Pliers, scissors, something like that. I imagine the Condemned who come through here have left all sorts of things lying about." I nod and begin searching the room as Grenda tries to comfort her sister.

"I wanted to ask you something," I say as I search several drawers.

"You're wondering why I asked you to come in here, right?"

"Well, yeah," I reply.

"I trust you more than the others," Grenda explains, "If you really are who I think you are, then I know I can trust you. I'm all the more certain since Jessica has taken an interest in you. That alone says plenty."

"Well...I'm glad I can help." I pull open one of the drawers and the front of it breaks off in my hand. A pair of pincers are sitting in the back of the drawer. They're rusty and corroded, but they should do the job.

"Here, try these." I toss the pincers to Grenda.

"Thanks." She begins snipping off the ends of the needles; each clipped piece falls to the floor with a faint tap of the hardwood.

"So..." Grenda says, "Do you think we'll get out of here?"

"I don't know," I admit, "It has to have been at least two hours by now. What did she say we had? A few hours to escape?"

"Yes, but that's a little vague," Grenda mumbles, clipping another needle, "Does that mean three hours? Four? Five? I think five is as far as I would go when saying a few."

"Plus it's not like I have a watch," I add, "Two is just a guess."

"I'd say two and half," Grenda replies, "I heard the clock tower chime on the hour twice already." I hear a knock on the door and go to answer it. Annie hands me a small roll of bandages and I thank her before closing the door.

"They found some?" Grenda asks.

"It would appear so."

"Well, since we're not removing the needles entirely, just hang on to them for now. I'll take them as soon as I'm finished. There's only a few more left. She's still a little out of it too. I'll try to get her to walk with me. Last thing I need is Genevieve complaining about how my sister is holding us up."

"Is she going to be okay?" I inquire.

"God, I hope so," Grenda quavers, "She's all I have. I really hate to ask Genevieve for help with this, but I'm afraid I'll have to. I can swallow my pride just this once...for my sister." The last piece of a severed needle falls to the floor and Grenda breathes a sigh of relief. The pincers fall to the floor with a clatter and she embraces her sister.

"It's going to be okay, Glenda," she sobs, "We're going to get out of here. Okay? Just hold on a little longer." I toss the roll of bandages to Grenda and get ready to leave the room. Without warning, Glenda lets out a blood curdling scream and grabs her sister by the throat with both hands. Grenda throws her off and tries to get away, but Glenda tackles her. Grenda screams as she lands on shards of broken glass and scattered pieces of debris. I try to pull Glenda off and she punches me in the nose. I hear Sybil shouting outside and turn to see her forcing her way into the room, knife drawn and ready to attack.

"I knew it!" Sybil screams, "I knew we couldn't trust those two!"

"Sybil, stop!" I cry, holding her back. She's in such a blind rage that it takes her a moment to realize what's happening.

"Get her off of me!" Grenda chokes. Sybil drops her knife and she and I each take one of Glenda's arms. We pull her off and Grenda wriggles free. She huddles in the corner, gasping for air.

"What the hell is wrong with her?" Sybil grunts. Glenda stomps on Sybil's foot and headbutts her in the nose, sending her reeling into the wall. She turns on me and begins punching me in the head and stomach. Sybil drags her to the floor. Genevieve tries to barge into the room, but I shoo her back out into the hall. The last thing we need is Glenda escaping. Sybil cries out in pain as Glenda elbows her in the cheek and stumbles to her feet. Grenda drags her back down, causing Glenda's head to thump against the floor. Grenda curses under her breath and helps her sister to her feet. Glenda teeters and stumbles backward into my arms. She's still conscious, but appears dazed. Sybil gets to her feet and glares at Glenda with a burning hatred. She swipes her knife off the floor and begins moving toward Glenda, only to be restrained by Grenda.

"She doesn't know what she's doing," Grenda explains, "She's not herself." Blood drips from Glenda's arms as she stares around the room. I glance down at the floor and see that something black is mixed in with her blood. Sybil's wounded hand is oozing something similar.

"Sybil...your hand," I say. Sybil looks down at her hand and back at me.

"What about it?" she shrugs.

"It looks infected with something," I reply, "Look, Glenda has it too. Look at her arms." Grenda and Sybil both examine Sybil's hand and Glenda's arm, but again they don't seem to take notice.

"What are you talking about?" Sybil asks with a look of concern.

"How can you not see that?"

"Are you sure you're okay, Wendy?" Grenda asks, "Glenda got you pretty good." I wipe some of the blood from my nose and see that it's all red. No black liquid anywhere to be seen. I jump in alarm as Glenda gasps and lets out a whimper.

"Glenda?" Grenda says, approaching her sister with caution. I look down at Glenda's arms to see that the black liquid is no longer oozing from her wounds, and neither is it mixed with the blood on the floor by my feet. Sybil still has some of it on her hand. I think back to what Valeska said. About how she had been reduced to a parasitic life form. She told me that one of my friends had found her. I shudder as I eye Sybil's hand. What should I do? What can I do? I'm the only one who can see it.

"How's it going in there?" Claire shouts from outside the door.

"We're coming out!" Sybil calls back. She motions for Grenda to help me move her sister out of the room. Sybil pushes some of the furniture out of the way and pulls the door open wide.

"What happened in there?" Genevieve asks.

"I don't know," Grenda admits, "Glenda just...lost it. I don't know why."

"I think she's fine now," I assure the others, "Let's get going."

"Right," Genevieve nods, "Let's get moving. Time is short." Sybil stumbles a little and leans against a wall for support. She coughs and continues walking. Only Annie and I take notice as the others hurry down the hallway.

"You sure you're okay to walk?" I ask Sybil. She nods and brushes past me. Annie gives a look of concern before following after her. I shake my head and hurry after the others. As I catch up to the group, I can't get what I saw out of my head.

Chapter 19

None of us say a word as we hurry down the streets, dodging Condemned as we go. Few give us trouble, and I hope it stays that way. We left the hospital about twenty minutes ago. We had to carry Claire and her wheelchair down separately, as well as help Glenda down the stairs, but so far neither of them have slowed us down. Sybil seems to be suffering from dizzy spells, something I expect is a result of our scuffle with Glenda. She hasn't said much, but she keeps insisting that she's fine. Glenda is starting to come to her senses and has begun to speak with her sister. The clock tower is only a short distance way. Soon we'll be back to the Plains. Assuming all goes according to plan.

"There it is, the clock tower," Claire observes, pointing to it.

"Looks like we're on the wrong side," Grenda says, "We're looking for 3:27, right?"

"Right," Genevieve confirms, "We go straight away from that clock face until we reach a tavern."

"Is there anything we should know about that place?" Tom asks.

"You mean like how it's often a powder keg filled with hostile Condemned?" Genevieve replies, "We should be fine as long as we can get into the basement without drawing attention."

"And how do you suggest we do that?" Claire demands, "In case you haven't noticed, we're not exactly prepared for a full scale brawl. If we stir up a crowd, we're not getting out of here at all."

"We'll be fine, I've done this before," Genevieve assures us.

"I hope you know what you're doing," I chime in.

"We'll head in through the back," Genevieve explains, "There's the back door everyone knows about, and there's a second one that I know about."

"You and how many others?" Claire mutters.

"The point is that we can use it to sneak into the storage room," Genevieve hisses, "From there it should be no problem getting into the basement."

The clock tower is only half a block away now. We're getting close. Genevieve leads us through an alley and around to the "3:27" side of the tower. Just as we're approaching the street, multiple gunshots can be heard, accompanied by the sound of rapid footsteps. We duck out of sight and wait for them to fade. As soon as the area goes silent, Genevieve leads us out into the street. A woman's body lies in a pool of blood nearby. A shotgun lies beside her.

"Someone get the shotgun," Genevieve orders, "Search the body for any extra shells." Sybil snatches up the shotgun and turns the body over. She finds a few shotgun shells, but leaves them in the woman's coat pocket. With some effort, she removes the woman's coat and puts it on."

"You didn't have to take the coat," Genevieve mutters while she and Tom begin moving the body into a nearby building.

"I needed the pockets!" Sybil snaps as she opens the shotgun and replaces the one spent shell, "Also, you don't need to move that body. It's not like we're trying to avoid arrest."

"I don't want her following us when she wakes up, you idiot," Genevieve snarls. She and Tom move the body into the building and out of sight. Sybil snorts in frustration and slings the shotgun over her shoulder. Moments later, Tom and Genevieve return and we all head to the tavern. As it comes into view, I see that it's a large brick building with a damaged sign dangling over the entrance. Genevieve guides us to the back of the building and begins searching behind a small shed. She returns seconds later with a key. I watch as she begins walking the length of the building, counting her steps under her breath. She stops at a point along the wall and begins counting a row of bricks. She places her palm against one and pushes it into the wall. Once it's been pushed back, she slides it to the left, revealing a keyhole. After using the key, she gives the wall a push with her shoulder, revealing a large portion of the wall to be a hidden door.

"Alright, get inside," Genevieve whispers over the sounds of rowdy patrons, "Stay in that room and wait for me." While she returns to the shed, the others and I file into the storage room and wait for her to come back. The storage room is nothing short of a mess, littered with both empty and broken bottles. It's difficult to move silently as we trudge through the room. It's dark except for the light of our lanterns. Claire struggles to stand with Tom and Annie helping her maintain her balance. There's no way we'll be able to move around the narrow corridors in this place with her in that wheelchair. She grimaces a little, but otherwise seems fine. Glenda is having her own troubles. She's awake enough to feel the pain from her wounds. She holds her arms close to her, occasionally cursing under her breath.

"Alright, listen up," Genevieve says, closing the door behind her, "I'll make this quick. Make sure you all stay hidden. Don't do anything that could attract attention to you."

"No need to state the obvious," Claire grumbles, "Who among us is really that dumb? I think we know what a danger Condemned are. We've all seen it." Genevieve rolls her eyes in frustration and continues.

"We're going to go one at a time into the rafters," Genevieve explains, pointing to a ladder in the far corner, "We'll do what we can to help the wounded. There's a hatch on the other side of the building, but this is the only way to get to it. You'll be able to see it once you're at the top of the ladder. Once inside, there's a staircase that will take you to the basement. You'll have to climb down out of the hatch, so again we'll need someone to help Claire and Glenda. There's a tunnel at the foot of the stairs. Follow it until you reach a gate and wait for me there. Everyone got it?"

Everyone nods. Genevieve stands guard near the door to the tavern interior and motions for us to start heading up the ladder. Grenda goes first. As soon as she vanishes at the top of the ladder, I go next. Once at the top, I can see down into the tavern. Ahead of me are a series of boards lain across the rafters to form a bridge. Grenda is on the other side, opening a small hatch in the wall. Glancing down into the tavern again, I see just how outnumbered we are. There must be at least fifty Condemned below me. My heart skips a beat as I notice one heading to the storage room. I turn back and wave frantically at the others.

"Someone is coming!" I mouth. Genevieve and Sybil both look up at me and shrug. Genevieve places a hand near her ear and insists that she can't hear. The storage room door swings open and Sybil panics. She raises her shotgun and fires, sending the man reeling into the hallway. A group of Condemned stands up at their table and a handful of others head toward the noise.

"You idiot!" Genevieve snarls as she hurries the others up the ladder, "Wendy, don't just sit there looking stupid! Get going!" I hurry across the boards, trying hard to keep from losing my balance. I just hope that no one has noticed what we're doing. If they start shooting, it's over. As I'm scrambling through the hatch, I notice that Glenda is right on my heels. Right as I climb down into the stairwell, I hear another shotgun blast and Genevieve and Sybil shouting. Glenda hops down and joins us, followed by Claire. Grenda and I catch her and help her balance on her uninjured leg. I can hear angry cries and screams echoing throughout the tavern. It sounds like tables and chairs are being overturned. I can hear people pounding on the storage room door. Glenda trots down the stairs and Grenda and I assist Claire.

"Why are you still here?" Genevieve shouts, clambering through the hatch, "Get going! We'll catch up!" Once at the foot of the stairs, I look back to see that Annie is climbing down from the hatch. That just leaves Tom and Sybil. Two more gunshots are heard and I feel my chest tighten. I just hope they can get to us alive. Genevieve herds us through the tunnel and toward the gate. Once we arrive at it, we wait for the others to catch up. More gunshots and screams echo from the tavern and I can feel myself beginning to panic.

"Open the gate!" I hear Sybil shriek, "Open it now! Hurry up!" Tom and Sybil come sprinting down the tunnel, the angry cries of Condemned behind them. They grow louder and louder as Sybil and Tom approach.

"They're right behind us!" Tom shouts. Genevieve turns, raises her rifle, and fires multiple rounds down the tunnel. The noise is deafening and leaves my ears ringing. Tom and Annie push the heavy steel gate open and begin beckoning us through.

"Come on!" Tom shouts as we file through. Genevieve and Sybil make a mad dash for the gate. Sybil turns and fires twice at the Condemned behind her. She then turns and bolts for the gate. The sound of another gunshot pierces the air. Sybil screams and falls to the ground in a heap, just short of the gate.

Chapter 20

"SYBIL!" I scream. Tom and I rush to help. I toss Sybil's shotgun to Grenda and Tom and I drag Sybil through the gate with only seconds to spare. Genevieve and Annie bolt the gate shut just as a horde of Condemned begin bashing their fists against it. Tom and I push two heavy barrels in front of it and turn our attention to Sybil.

"Stay with us, Sybil!" Genevieve says while I help Sybil onto Tom's back.

"How much further?" Tom grunts.

"Not far," Genevieve replies, "Once we reach the end of this tunnel, we'll be close by. Just make sure Sybil stays conscious. Someone put pressure on her wound."

"Wendy, catch!" Grenda calls to me as she tosses me the roll of bandages from the hospital. I thank her and follow behind Tom. Blood is seeping from just beneath the bottom of Sybil's coat. It looks like she's been hit in her pelvis. It's very difficult to do, but I unravel some of the bandages and press them to Sybil's wound. I try to keep pressure on it as best I can, but she's bouncing around too much.

"What's my name, Sybil?" Tom asks as we continue through the tunnel.

"Tom..." she mumbles.

"What's your name?" he asks.

"Sybil, you idiot..." she mutters.

"He's just trying to keep you engaged, Sybil," I explain, "Keep it up."

"Not much further now. She'll be fine the second she gets back to the Plains," Genevieve cuts in, "Just keep at it a little longer." Several tense minutes tick by as Tom and I work to prevent Sybil from bleeding out. I don't say anything to anyone, but the black liquid I saw at the hospital is now mixed in with the blood on the bandages. Sybil remains conscious, but it's clear that she's losing strength. The tunnel narrows and changes from stone to wood. Not long after that, I can see two lanterns marking the exit. It seems so far, yet so close. I almost feel as though time is slowing down. I can see a shadowy figure standing at the end of the tunnel, but it's only there for a few seconds, vanishing in the blink of an eye. For a moment, I almost hope it's Reika waiting to assist us and not something worse. We can't take anymore hits. Next time one of us might get killed. The tunnel ends and we come into a small clearing in the middle of a wooded area. I glance through the trees behind us and see lights in the distance. It looks like we're just outside the city.

"This is it," Genevieve pants. Tom is so exhausted that he can barely stand. I help Sybil off his back and lay her down on her stomach. She groans as she turns her head to the side and I resume putting pressure on her wound. I watch as Genevieve frantically searches around a large tree with a swing hanging from one of the branches.

"I left it right here!" she panics, "I know I did! I knew something like this might happen again and I left a key here just in case."

"What?" Claire shouts, "You can't find the key?"

"Just give me a second!" Genevieve snaps. She continues searching around the base of the tree. She stops, circles around to the front of the tree, and lets out a frustrated groan.

"Are you sure it's there?" Tom asks.

"I thought it was," Genevieve answers, "This is ridiculous! I know it was here! I know it!"

"Well, tell me where to look and I'll help!" Tom barks, beginning his search near the tree. Genevieve lets out a frustrated snarl and pushes him away from the tree.

"If I can't find it, then I'm sure you won't either!" she snaps, stamping her foot in frustration.

"You don't have to look for it by yourself," Tom insists, "We're all panicking and we would do good to have more than one pair of eyes searching for it."

"It's not here, Tom!" Genevieve insists, "We're finished! Someone must have taken it!"

"Yeah, good idea, Genevieve!" Claire chimes in, "Let's give up and let our friend die and become trapped here! Stop acting like you have to do everything on your own and just let him help you!"

"Shut it, Claire!" Genevieve hisses, "I can't think with you hollering at me!"

"You got us this far," Glenda cuts in, "We're a team whether or you like it or not! Now let's hurry up and find the key!"

"I'm telling you, it's not here!" Genevieve shouts, "Go on! Have a look for yourself!"

"Tom, just go look for the damn thing!" Grenda orders, "Don't let her push you around, I don't care if she is a former gatekeeper."

"What does my history have to do with this?" Genevieve demands.

"Because you think you're superior to the rest of us!" Grenda hollers.

"All of you shut up and do something!" I scream, "Sybil's dying and you're standing around arguing! Why don't you spend what little time we have left figuring out a solution!" Everyone goes silent as I glare at them. Sybil coughs and blood drips from her mouth. Genevieve opens her mouth to speak. In the dim light I can see her expression shift from anger to terror. Angry shrieks echo from the tunnel and I turn to see a horde of Condemned rushing straight toward us. Within seconds, they've reached the mouth of the tunnel. They're on us so fast that none of us have time to react.

"That's enough!" booms a woman's voice from nearby. The others and I all turn to see a hooded woman emerging from the trees. Beside her is Reika. The Condemned all back away from us, each of them staring at the hooded woman.

"Reika?" I gasp, "What's going on?" The hooded woman raises one of her skeletal hands in front of her. Clutched between her fingers is a small black orb, much like the one Linda used to send us here. That must be the key Genevieve was looking for.

"Hello again, Wendy," Reika smiles, waving as she speaks.

"I knew it..." Genevieve growls, "She was following us..." The woman beside Reika pockets the orb and pulls back her hood. I can see at once that she has long white hair and dark skin. Her face is boney and harsh. Her irises are a deep, glowing purple, and her scelras black as the darkness that surrounds us. Her feet are visible beneath her long, black robes. They're both mere bone, just like her hands. She glares at the many Condemned who surround us.

"All but the intruders, will kneel at once!" she bellows. One by one, each of the Condemned lay down their weapons and kneel. Each of them bow their heads and hold perfectly still.

"I'm afraid none of you will be going anywhere," the woman growls, "No one leaves the Abyss without my consent. You were all fools to try. As for you Genevieve...I'm rather fed up with your visits to my realm.

You know Shadows aren't welcome here. Perhaps if you enjoy it here so much, you should stay."

"It's tempting, but I'll pass..." Genevieve replies.

"Watch your mouth," the woman hisses.

"That key is the property of the Midnight Council," Genevieve continues, "You have no right to touch it."

"I have more right to do so than a former gatekeeper," the woman snarls. She storms over to Genevieve and grabs her by the throat, "This key was left in my realm...so it is mine to do with as I please. Just like the lot of you." She hurls Genevieve to the ground and glares at her.

"We're under council protection," Genevieve grunts, getting to her feet, "There will be hell to pay if you don't let us go, Lydia." Genevieve lets out a yelp as Lydia strikes her across the cheek.

"Insolent wretch!" Lydia rages, "I am Queen Lydia of the Abyss, and you will address me as 'your highness.' Got that?" Genevieve stares defiantly at Lydia. A bruise is visible on her cheek.

"The council has power over a realm only if that realm's Queen grants it to them," Lydia explains, "Since I granted no such authority to the council, you remain under my rule while in this realm."

"Maris granted her authority to the council," Genevieve snarls, "Her power surpasses your own! You'll be answering to her if you don't let us leave!" Lydia hurls Genevieve into a nearby tree with tremendous force. She falls to the ground in a heap while the others look on in horror.

"How dare you threaten me?" Lydia seethes. She reaches down and drags Genevieve to her feet. "A few days in the Witherlands should straighten you out."

"Get away from her!" I shout. Lydia turns her head and glares at me. She lets go of Genevieve and storms over to me.

"Congratulations, child!" Lydia hisses, "You get to go with her." I stand up and see that she's several inches taller than me. I glare up at her, not caring about what she might do. I need to get Sybil out of here and she's in my way.

"You're a living soul..." Lydia whispers, placing her boney hand on my cheek, "Strange...how did you get here? Explain yourself."

"I want that key..." I growl.

"And I want an explanation!" Lydia hisses, clamping her hand down on my arm, "Now...what's your name?" I can feel an intense, withering cold spreading from her palm.

"Wendy..." I sneer, "Wendy Warland." Lydia's expression changes from one of menace, to one of confusion.

"Wendy Warland?" she repeats. She loosens her grasp and the cold sensation vanishes, "You're alive. You look younger than I remember. How very curious. I suppose it makes sense, though. Given the circumstances."

"What are you talking about?" I demand.

"It's nothing," Lydia replies, "Just a simple misunderstanding." She steps back and snaps her fingers. The others and I watch as the Condemned all rise to their feet in unison and file back into the tunnel.

"I don't much care for Shadows invading my realm," Lydia continues, "I sent Reika to keep an eye on you all. When any soul, Shadow, Luminary, Condemned, any of them...leave my realm, I find it insulting. This is supposed to be a hellish place of existence, from which there is no escape. No one leaves unless I say so. Only I come and go as I please."

"I never asked for your permission," I snarl.

"Calm yourself, Wendy," Lydia replies. She removes the key from her pocket and places it in my hand, then closes her hands around mine, "I'll make an exception for you and the others, but don't mistake my kindness for weakness. I have my reasons for doing you this favor. I'm sure I don't need to tell any of you that this place is dangerous, and that coming back would be unwise. Now...take this and go," Lydia urges, "Sybil has little time left. If she dies here, even I will not be able to undo her fate. She will be bound here forever. It is simply the nature of the Abyss." She lets go and I step back, my hands are as cold as ice. I turn and toss the key to a surprised Genevieve who looks on in confusion.

"Don't just stand there, get the gate open!" I shout. Genevieve nods and hurries to the ravine.

"Come on!" Genevieve calls, motioning for the others to follow. Claire climbs onto Tom's back and Annie and Grenda work together to carry Sybil. I turn back to Lydia and glance past her at Reika. She waves and smiles.

"I assume Reika didn't cause you any problems?" Lydia cuts in.

"None at all. She helped me out on my way here," I reply.

"You did what?" Lydia thunders, turning to face Reika.

"I was just following orders," Reika shrugs.

"Until now, I thought she was a rogue!" Lydia snarls, "I never told you to lend any assistance! What if they had been someone else?"

"Maris requested that I assist them," Reika explains, "She told me not to tell you. She didn't want you to get too involved for some reason."

"I see..." Lydia says, "She thinks I'll say too much, doesn't she? Typical..." She looks back at me and places her hands on my shoulders.

"It's good to see you again, Wendy," Lydia smiles, "Now...get going. Don't make the others wait for you." I turn and start toward the gate in the distance, but I stop before I take more than a few steps.

"Who are you?" I ask.

"The ruler of the Abyss, of course," Lydia replies.

"No, that's not what I mean," I say, turning to face her, "Who are you, really? And why are you helping us?" Lydia smiles and motions for me to follow her to the gate.

"I can't tell you everything, Wendy," Lydia explains, "but I can tell you that you and I have met before. You've been here before. Not just once...but many times."

"I have?" I whisper. Lydia nods.

"Maybe once this is all over, you can come visit me again. I'm always happy to see my little sister." My eyes widen. This must be who Jessica was referring to in my dream.

"Go..." Lydia urges, giving me a light push, "You and I will meet again soon. When the day you want to seek me out arrives, you'll know just how to do so." I turn and glance at her one last time. We lock eyes for a moment and I turn to face the gate. I make a mad dash for the gate and slow to a jog near the edge of the ravine. I can see a small pathway leading to the gate.

"Hurry up!" Genevieve shouts, gesturing for me to follow her through. She vanishes through the gate and I take one last look behind me. I can see Reika and Lydia watching me. After turning back to face the gate, I take a deep breath and dash through it.

Chapter 21

Everything has gone dark and I feel like I'm falling. I can feel myself slowing down and soon I come to a stop. I can smell smoke and hear the crackling of flames. My eyes snap open and I'm lying face down on the floor of my room. As I'm getting up, I notice something strange. My scars are gone. My hands and forearms look as though they were never burned.

"What's going on?" I whisper. As I get to my feet, I can hear the flicker of flames beyond the door. While I'm glancing at my surroundings, I notice my reflection in the mirror. I'm my normal sixteen-year-old self. No sign of the older self I sometimes see. I look down at my hands and then at my reflection. This can't be right. When was there ever a fire at Red Oak? A scream breaks the silence and I rush to the door. It's Annie. I pull the door open and smoke pours into the room. Just before I step into the hall, a wooden beam crashes down in front of me. I yelp and jump back in alarm. Is this real? Am I back at the orphanage? The heat is so intense it it makes me cringe. The smoke is stinging my eyes and I can barely see. I duck down and crawl under some of the fallen debris. Annie is screaming for help somewhere up ahead. With the flames roaring around me, I continue working my way toward the dining hall. The smoke is getting thicker. I continue through the inferno as fast as I can. My heart pounds as I listen for Annie.

I hear her call out again. My foot catches on a piece of debris and I stumble forward. I land on my forearms and pull myself back onto my knees. Something crashes in the next room. Part of the ceiling must have given way. I hadn't even thought about the roof caving in. Fallen debris blocks most of the doorway to the dining hall. Seconds tick by and she calls out again. I try my hardest to squeeze through the doorway, but it begins to collapse as I crawl through. Just as I stumble inside, I'm knocked to the ground. My leg is pinned under several flaming pieces of debris. Annie calls out again and this time I can tell she's nearby. She's in this room, but the smoke is too thick to see her.

"Annie!" I shout. There's nothing but the roar of the inferno around me. I try to pull my leg loose, but it won't budge. The flames spread closer and I begin to panic. Annie screams and I grab hold of the chunk of wood trapping my leg. I recoil as soon as I touch it. With a deep breath I make a second attempt. This time I maintain my hold. The flames scorch my hands and forearms. I scream in pain, but I refuse to let go. With every ounce of strength I can muster, I manage to free my foot. I stumble to my feet holding my hands close to my stomach. With my teeth gritted, I press on.

"Annie!" I shout, "Where are you?" I hear her shout for me and I race to find her. She's pinned under a large beam. Both of her legs are trapped and she's trying to pull herself free. She spots me and reaches out to me.

"Wendy, thank God!" she cries, "Get me out of here!" She takes my hand and I try to pull her free. She screams in pain and I let go, my hands aching worse than ever. I don't want to look, but I can feel pieces of skin coming loose. Even if I manage to free her, I'll still have to carry her out. A piece of bone is jutting from her shin. I try to lift the beam pinning her, but I can barely move it. The flames scorch my hands even more and it becomes harder to maintain my grip.

"Just a little more!" Annie grunts, "I'm almost free!" I use every ounce of strength in my body, but I can't lift the beam much more than a few inches. Without warning, a hand grabs me by the arm and I'm hurled to the ground. One of my hands strikes the floor in the fall and I scream in pain. I look up to see a cloaked woman standing before me. The lower half of her face is covered and all I can see beneath the hood is a single coal black eye. Her long, black hair hangs over shoulders. In her hand is a large dagger. The weapon looks as though it's comprised of black smoke. She crouches in front of me and grabs me by the hair. I scream in pain as the blade pierces my chest multiple times. The woman turns and approaches Annie.

"Back off!" I scream, "Get away from her!" Annie screams and the woman sinks the knife into her body. Annie's screams cease in an instant. With blood dripping from my mouth and pooling beneath me, I force myself to my feet. I'm struggling to breathe, but I'm so enraged that I can't feel any pain. The woman turns and takes one last look at me. I start coughing and blood spatters on the floor in front of me. My knees quake and I gasp for air.

"I'll kill you!" I shriek. Using the last of my strength, I charge at her. She doesn't even move, just glares at me from under that hood. I slam my fist into her jaw. She does little more than flinch. My eyes widen as her knife pierces my stomach. Blood spills onto the floor and I feel my legs begin to quiver and weaken. She pulls the blade loose and I collapse beside Annie's body. The woman stares down at me, then turns and vanishes through a wall of flames. I can hear voices nearby. The front doors swing open and the sound of footsteps reach my ears. The voices are louder now, but I can't make out what they're saying. My vision fades just as someone finds me. The voices are blending together and fading fast. Soon, nothing but darkness remains. My eyes snap open and I gasp for air. I'm back in the Plains, lying in the ship-yard where the others and I first encountered Linda. Sybil, Annie, and Genevieve are kneeling beside me.

"Where is everyone?" I ask.

"Never mind that," Sybil replies, "Are you okay? You passed out."

"I think so," I mumble. I sit up and they help me to my feet.

"Think you can walk?" Genevieve asks me.

"Where is everyone?" I ask again.

"They left to go find help," Sybil explains as she motions for me to follow her and Annie, "Come on, we can't stay here. We need to get you and Annie back to Red Oak."

Chapter 22

Genevieve lets out a yelp as I pin her against a nearby wall.

"You're working with her, aren't you?" I snarl, "She tried to kill me!" I turn and glance at Annie. She backs away and sprints away from us.

"Annie!" Sybil shouts. Genevieve pushes me off and runs after her. They both vanish around a corner.

"You remembered, didn't you?" Sybil asks.

"She's dead..." I quaver, "She's been dead this whole time..." Sybil turns and embraces me in a tight hug.

"I'm sorry we couldn't tell you..." she says.

"Then that means Jessica did try to kill me," I hiss. I throw Sybil off and she stumbles backward. Tears are forming in her eyes.

"No, no, Wendy you've got it all wrong," she replies, "It wasn't Jessica! I swear!"

"Get away from me!" I scream. I can't believe this. Valeska was right. Jessica made an attempt on my life. Sybil betrayed me! Right as I round the corner, I crash into someone. I stumble back and almost lose my balance. It's Jessica.

"Hello, Wendy," she smiles. I sneer and try to walk past her. She grabs my arm and holds me in place.

"Is something wrong?" she asks. Sybil catches up and I hear her stop several feet behind me. I yank my arm loose and turn to face them.

"I know what happened," I growl, "You're name isn't Jessica...it's Maris...and you killed my friend!"

"You're half right," Maris replies, "I am Maris...but I'm afraid you're mistaken about Annie."

"Liar!" I scream, "You wanted me dead! Valeska told me everything!" Maris's eyes widen.

"What did you just say?"

"Valeska! My sister!" I shout.

"I had hoped you would never meet her," Maris replies, "Whatever she told you was a lie. She can't be trusted. There's a reason I dethroned her. She went wild, out of control, she wrought havoc in the afterlife realms."

"Do you really expect me to trust you?" I snarl, "I know what I saw! I saw you kill Annie right in front of me! I don't care about what you did to me! You brought my friend into this! I'll never forgive you for that!"

"And you won't have to," Sybil cuts in. Sybil's usual red eyes have turned yellow like Valeska's. She snaps her fingers and dozens of chains spring forth from the ground. They ensnare Maris and drag her to her knees.

"Valeska!" she screams, struggling to get loose. Valeska steps in front of Maris and grabs hold of her throat with both hands. Maris screams in agony and begins to wither before my eyes. Her eyes become sunken, her face gaunt, and her hair turns white as snow. Valeska stands up and the chains fade away.

"Same trick you used on me, you old hag," she mutters, "Remember that?" She kicks Maris in the stomach and we both watch her fall onto her side.

"Petulant child!" Maris snarls, "How dare you?" Valeska smirks and digs the heel of her boot into Maris's cheek.

"I'm only doing what you won't," Valeska growls, "The four realms will soon see the rise of a new era." She removes her boot and steps back.

"You've sunken to a new low," Maris hisses as she pulls herself onto her knees, "I should've dealt with you properly...the first time this happened. You'll regret dragging Wendy into this...that much I can assure you..."

"Is that supposed to be a threat?" Valeska snorts. She holds out her palm and a swirling black portal opens behind Maris. Over a dozen shadowy arms reach out and take hold of her.

"Arrogant...just like your father..." Maris growls, glaring at Valeska, "You're making a grave mistake and you don't even realize it..." Valeska stoops down in front of Maris and scowls at her in silence. She slaps Maris across the face and grabs her by the front of her coat.

"I don't make mistakes..." Valeska whispers, "Not anymore..." She stands up and snaps her fingers. The arms begin pulling Maris into the portal. She struggles against them right up until she's pulled through.

"You're wrong, Valeska!" Maris shouts. She vanishes and the portal closes up. Valeska and I are left alone. She turns, picks me up in a bear hug, and spins me around.

"We're finally free of that wretch!" she squeals as she puts me down, "I never thought this day would arrive. There's just one last thing we need to do. Find Linda before she does any lasting damage."

"What's going to happen to Sybil?" I ask.

"Who cares?" Valeska snorts.

"I'm just wondering why you still look like her," I reply.

"I'm afraid I'm still weak from being imprisoned for so long," she explains, "I'll be back to my old self soon enough." She holds her palm out in front of her and another portal opens a few feet from us.

"Come on," she says, motioning for me to follow, "We need to get you back to Red Oak."

"What does it matter?" I ask, "It's not even real, is it?"

"We need to hurry, Wendy. Just trust me, I know what I'm doing." I take a step forward and hesitate. Valeska grabs my arm and pulls me through the portal.

Chapter 23

The portal drops us just outside of the orphanage. Valeska and I race up the steps and crash through the front doors.

"Where are we going?" I ask.

"Where's the door you used to come here?"

"It's upstairs." I lead her up the staircase and to the fourth floor. I point out the door, and she places her hand against it. The door becomes engulfed and swings open. The two of us step through and Valeska closes the door behind us.

"Before we go any further, I want to know what's going on," I say, "Nothing about this makes any sense! If what I saw in that dream was true, and it seems it is, then this place burned down." Valeska places her hands on my shoulders and looks me in the eye.

"I'll make it quick," she says, taking a deep breath, "You're asleep, but you're also awake. Your body is at rest, your spirit is not. That said, this is not a dream. Everything else you've experienced has been real. The Ashen Plains, your friends, Linda and the others, the Abyss, all of it; but this city...it's not the real Cinder Valley."

"Then what is it?" Why am I getting a bad feeling all of a sudden? Something about the way she's looking at me is making me uneasy.

"This is a memory, Wendy. An illusion you created within your own mind. This is how the orphanage was when you were sixteen, shortly before it caught fire. Years later, you were severely injured in an accident and lapsed into a coma. Understand?"

"The train..." I whisper.

"That's right," she confirms, "This, everything you see now, is your own mind. That's why your friends told you that you're vulnerable. If your mind incurs too much damage, you'll never wake up from your coma. You'll die in your sleep. These people you see, the wards, the townspeople...they're only memories. But none of that matters anymore. Your usefulness ends here."

"My what?" I gasp, taking a step back, "What are you saying?"

"I'm saying I don't need you anymore!" Valeska laughs, "I can't even tell you how relieved I was to discover that you'd lost your memory.

The perfect pawn for the perfect plan." She lets out a cackle and slowly, her appearance changes back to normal. She stares down at me from her slightly greater height and clamps her hands around my throat.

"Now that Maris is gone and Sybil is no more, all that's left is to get rid of you," she whispers with a malicious grin, "But don't worry...it's for a good cause." She lets go long enough to punch me in the cheek and I find myself on the floor, too disoriented to stand. She throws open a window and drags me toward it. I struggle to get free, but she smashes my head against the windowsill. The next thing I know I'm looking down at the courtyard with blood dripping from my nose and lip.

"It was nice meeting you, Wendy," Valeska cackles, "See you on the other side!" Despite my attempts to get loose, she hurls me out the window and toward the pavement. I clip a nearby tree on the way down and land in a heap beside it. The world goes dark in an instant, but I'm not out for long. Soon I hear an unfamiliar voice calling to me.

"Wendy? Wendy wake up!" My eyes snap open. A black-haired woman with brown eyes and skin is kneeling beside me. She looks to be of Native American descent. Standing beside the woman is Annie.

"I see you've met your sister," the woman grunts, helping me to my feet, "Can you stand?"

"Who are you?" I mumble, still struggling to see straight.

"Chloe," she replies, "Chloe Cavallini. We don't have a lot of time for introductions, so you're just going to have to trust me."

"She's Valeska's sentinel," Annie explains, "She followed us from the shipyard." I shove Chloe back and step away from her.

"You're with her!" I snarl, "You're with Valeska!" I draw my revolver and point it at her heart.

"No, no, I assure you I'm not!" Chloe assures me. I can see now that she's holding a Civil War era revolver in one hand. On her hip is a holster and around her waist is a belt with multiple spare cylinders.

"How am I still alive?" I grunt, lowering my aching arm, "How can I even stand after that?" Pieces of my shattered memory are returning. The Sentinels...I remember now. There are four of them. Sybil, Reika, and another one...in the Oasis...I can't remember her name. This woman in front of me...she's not her. She's the fourth one I never met. The one that disappeared after Valeska's defeat.

"Why are you here?" I demand, "Why now? No one's seen you in years."

"I'll explain as we go, but we need to find your sister," Chloe urges. I nod and take a few steps forward. My legs ache and fight against me as I go. I'm starting to remember a little more. As I'm following Chloe and Annie toward the nearest entrance, a series of flashbacks fill my mind. I'm remembering Sybil telling me I'm Maris's daughter at the age of eighteen, when she told me she had been assigned to watch over me until I came of age, and even the visits to the Abyss that Lydia told me about.

My injuries slow me down enough for Chloe and Annie to enter the building before me. Neither of them look back, assuming I'm right on their tail. My vision goes blurry for a moment and returns to normal as I grasp the door handle. When I step inside, I'm greeted with an abandoned and dilapidated hallway. The screams I heard only moments before can no longer be heard and Chloe and Annie are nowhere to be seen. Up ahead are two figures, both of whom I recognize. One of them is me and the other is Sybil. I blink several times and continue down the hallway. At first I'm confused, but soon I begin to remember. This was a year after the fire. Sybil took me back here after Annie died. My wounds had healed and I was struggling to cope with what happened. I reach down, pick up a small piece of wood, and toss it in their direction. Neither of them take notice. It's as I suspected, they can't see or hear me.

"Sybil..." I whisper, "I'm going to fix this...I promise..." I can't hear what either of them are saying. It's like a radio getting poor reception. I can hear bits and pieces, but nothing coherent. What else was she telling me? I can't remember. Light begins to flood the hallway through a nearby window and soon it's too bright to see. When the light dims, I can see that the room has changed. I'm in a hospital now. My doppelganger is lying unconscious in the bed before me. I can feel my heart beginning to pound. Her arms are bandaged and Sybil is pacing back and forth with her face buried in her hands. I can hear her sobbing. More light pours in and again it fades to reveal a new location. This time I'm at a train station. I can see myself about twenty feet away where I'm in line for a ticket. I look tired...like I haven't slept in ages. Her hair is unkempt and her face stained with tears. Sybil is nowhere to be seen.

"I said something to her..." I murmur, "She left me. Where is this... where am I? Why was I here? Why did Sybil leave?" My head begins to ache and soon it becomes unbearable. I grab the sides of my head and fall to my knees. I look up for a moment and see that I'm now in the compartment on the train. A number twenty-three is written in blood on the window, and a twenty-five is scrawled in black ink on the adjacent wall.

"What is this? What's going on?" My vision fades, then comes back into focus. I'm back at the orphanage, on my knees and slumped against the door with my hand still grasping the handle. I stand up as the sound of screams reaches my ears. It seemed like much longer, but I must have been out for only a few seconds. I fling the door open to find the broken bodies of two wards lying nearby. The walls and floor around them are covered in blood. Gunshots are erupting from the dining hall ahead of me. With my revolver in hand, I sprint toward the sounds, dodging fleeing wards and staff while stepping over the bodies of others. Upon entering the dining hall, I can see that the floor is littered with over a dozen slain wards. Blood is splattered all over the floor and across tables and walls. Some people are still running out of the dining hall in a panic. Among the chaos, I see a trail of black blood leading to the front doors. Genevieve races toward the front entrance and Chloe is standing in the middle of the room speaking with Annie. My eyes widen in horror as I observe the carnage before me.

"Wendy!" Annie exclaims, running to my side, "Wendy, come on, we have to keep moving!"

"This is all my fault..." I murmur. Annie takes my arm and pulls me along.

"Hurry up!" Annie urges, "You've gotta snap out of it! These aren't real people!" Slowly, bit by bit, my shock is being replaced by an overwhelming anger. I clench my fists and race past Chloe and Annie. They both call after me, but I don't listen. I burst through the front doors and sprint down the street, following the traces of blood. As I'm racing down the street, more memories flash through my head. The first time I remember meeting Sybil, the days after my aunt and uncle died, the years I spent in Red Oak, the time I spent in the hospital. She never left my side...not until the weeks leading up to the train station. It had something to do with her past. I shamed her for it, I told her to stay away from me. I called her a monster. But why? Why would I say that to her? The blood trail leads me down an alley and toward the back door of a deserted shop. I slow to a halt near the door and listen for any signs of movement inside. Chloe and Annie are going to catch up to me any moment now. Still panting, I clutch my revolver in one hand and give the door a light push. It creaks open and I spot Genevieve lying face-down on the floor.

Chapter 24

"Genevieve!" I exclaim, "Genevieve! Wake up!" I roll her over and she groans in pain. Her nose is broken and her cheek is gashed open and bleeding. She opens her eyes and pushes me away.

"I'm fine," Genevieve grunts, getting to her feet, "I managed to slow her down a little...but not much else."

"Where did she go?" I demand.

"She ran off a few minutes ago," Genevieve answers, getting to her feet, "Linda was here too." She pauses for a moment and the both of us listen. I can hear rapid footsteps approaching the shop. Seconds later, Annie and Chloe enter the shop, both out of breath and panting.

"What the hell were you thinking?" Chloe pants, glaring at me, "Why'd you leave us behind like that?"

"She tried to help me," Genevieve grunts, clutching her bleeding arm, "I don't know why. Valeska chased her out of here."

"Who?" Chloe inquires.

"Linda," Genevieve answers.

"She what?" Annie asks, "Why would Linda try to help you?"

"Your guess is as good as mine," Genevieve shrugs, "All I know is Valeska was furious with her."

"For helping you?" I ask.

"Sounded like there was more to it than that," Genevieve explains, "I didn't catch much of it. All I know is she stole my rifle and most of my ammo." Multiple gunshots ring out down the street.

"That must be her," Chloe mutters, brushing past me. The four of us exit the shop and head out onto the street. Another gunshot cuts through the air. Linda stumbles from around a corner and begins racing down the street toward us. Just behind her is Valeska, calmly striding after her.

"Sneaky little brat..." Valeska growls. People along the street are scattering. Some huddle behind cars and watch the scene unfold.

"I'm sorry! I just thought-" Linda panics.

"Thought what?" Valeska rages, "Thought you could stab me in the back?" She fires at Linda, striking her in the arm. She screams and falls to the ground, blood spattering the pavement.

"I was only making a head start! I was just doing what you told me to do!"

"I've heard enough!" Valeska rages. She holds out her palm, the same way she did when she summoned the portal that brought us here. To my surprise, nothing happens. She tries again, but still nothing. Linda spots me and the others.

"Help me!" she screams, "Please! You have to help me!" Valeska turns her attention to me as I approach Linda, my revolver clutched in my hand.

"Unbelievable..." Valeska growls, lowering her weapon, "Why can't you do your big sister a favor and just die already?" I glare at Valeska, then down at Linda.

"Please help me!" Linda begs, stumbling to her feet. She sprints forward and stands cowering behind me. I turn and shove her to the ground.

"You're really going to ask me for help?" I rage, pointing my revolver at her forehead, "Did you already forget the role you played in all of this?"

"Please, I can explain, just give me a chance!" Linda pleads. Before I can pull the trigger, Valeska does it herself. Linda is struck in the side of the head, splattering the pavement with blood. She falls to her side and her body quickly disintegrates into a pile of ash.

"I think we've both heard enough out of her," Valeska mutters, lowering her weapon.

"What was she going to say, Valeska?" I demand.

"Hell if I know," Valeska laughs, "What do you care, anyway? She was nothing but trash. A rat, a crook, a tool I no longer needed."

"Maris was right to lock you away," I growl, taking a few paces toward her, "You're nothing but a monster." Valeska giggles and comes closer.

"Aren't we both monsters? Think about it, Wendy. You and I have the same blood. We're the daughters of Maris herself...but we're also half-human. So what does that make us? Hmm?"

"This isn't about blood," I hiss.

"Then what is it about, Wendy?" Valeska snarls, "Is it about who I am and how I do things? Or is it more about you and your own naive sense of justice? This is why I can't let you live. If you do, you'll rule over the Ashen Plains someday. That's something I simply cannot allow. The spirits who reside in the Plains require a firm hand to guide them, to keep them in line; not some silly, hopeless little girl whose head is brimming with idealistic nonsense!"

"Don't you dare talk down to me!" I snap, "You're a filthy coward, a murderer! You've got innocent blood on your hands!"

"You're going to have all kinds of fun when your memory returns," Valeska sneers, "You really think you're innocent? You think you're better than me? That you've never done anything terrible? Well let me tell you something you little shit! You've got just as much blood on you! I am only doing what's necessary! Leaving Maris in power would have been unacceptable. Sometimes change demands blood, it demands sacrifice!"

"I may not remember everything yet, but I know I wouldn't walk into an orphanage and butcher two wards after setting it ablaze!" I snarl, shoving her backward. She barely moves and proceeds to backhand me across the face. She then grabs me by the collar of my dress and narrows her eyes.

"I will never understand how you could be so upset over the death of a lowly human," Valeska growls, "You killed plenty of humans, people who deserved death, but you don't remember! Annie was nothing, Wendy. She's nothing but another soul to reap. She would have been crippled for life after what happened to her leg! I spared her that suffering! What does it matter when a human dies? That's what humans are made to do. Live short, pathetic little lives, expire, and spend eternity under our rule."

"Is that was Chloe was to you?" I snort, "Another soul to reap? Maybe I do have blood on my hands, maybe I don't remember, maybe I will be in for a shock when those memories return...but what I do know is this. There are good people in this world, just as there are evil ones. I cannot bring myself to believe that every human is terrible, it just isn't true! You're by far the most wicked person I've ever met and you're only half! So what's your excuse? Annie is my friend, Sybil, Genevieve, all of them. If I did make mistakes in the past, I will right those wrongs in the future, but I will not blame my enemies for how I choose to conduct myself. If you can't see that, then how can you ever hope to be a leader? Don't you feel we have a responsibility to lead by example?"

"Is that what you think?" Valeska rages, "You listen to me and you listen well! It's that sort of naive thinking that makes leaders weak! Compassion can be allowed no place your heart! Never show weakness! Never give your enemies a chance to take advantage of you!"

"Humans are not your enemy!" I argue.

"I disagree..." Valeska snarls. She shoves me to the ground, raises her rifle, and fires a single shot. I look up to see Chloe collapsing to the pavement. Valeska lets out a cackle and fires at Annie and Genevieve. Annie falls to the ground in a heap, her body turning to ash seconds later. Genevieve is struck in the hip and stumbles. She darts into an alley, another round sailing into the wall behind her. Valeska stomps her foot on my back before I can get up, pinning me to the ground. I struggle to reach my revolver, but it's just out of my reach. I can feel my heart racing in my chest.

"This is where it ends, Wendy," Valeska growls, "I sat rotting in the Abyss for decades, just waiting for this moment. That train wreck was a blessing. Say hello to Lydia for me..." I cringe and close my eyes. A gunshot rings out and I open them again. Valeska drops her rifle and it clatters on the pavement beside me. She lets out an angry shriek and removes her foot from my back. I snatch up my revolver and scramble to my feet. Chloe is struggling to stand up and clutching her ribs. Blood is seeping through her clothes and between her fingers.

"Chloe!" Valeska screams. Chloe lowers her weapon and I hear footsteps behind me. Genevieve races past me and slams a crowbar into Valeska's shoulder. She lets out a scream and stumbles backward. Chloe discards the empty cylinder and replaces it. Valeska and Genevieve begin struggling for control of the crowbar and soon Valeska rips it from her hands. Genevieve dodges several vicious swings and attempts to take the crowbar back. Valeska shoves her into a car and smashes the crowbar across her face. She falls to the ground, eyes wide open and dead before she hits the ground.

"Genevieve!" I scream. I fire all six rounds at Valeska, striking her in the chest, stomach and thigh. Two rounds sail past her and embed in a nearby building. The cloudy skies above begin to darken and lightning flashes in the distance. A deafening roar of thunder soon follows. The few dozen people fleeing the scene begin to fade away and soon they vanish like ghosts. Genevieve's body turns to ash and washes away with the rain. Valeska charges toward me and slams the crowbar into my stomach. I double over in pain and drop to my knees, the wind knocked clean out of me. She goes after Chloe who fires twice and takes off running back toward the orphanage with Valeska in tow. After a few moments, I manage a ragged breath and stumble to my feet. I hear two more gunshots and struggle to move faster. There's no telling how much longer Chloe can hold her off.

The further I move down the street, the more dilapidated the structures become. Windows are smashed out, some boarded up. Vehicles parked along the street are rusting and falling apart. Soon the orphanage comes into view. Much of the building is scorched and other areas are overgrown and tangled with plant life. I follow a trail of blood up the steps and into the building. I push the door open and hear another gunshot. I empty the spent cartridges from my weapon and replace them as fast as I can. That may have been Chloe's last round. I can't assume that she'll be able to reload on the run. I grip the revolver in my hand and take a deep breath.

Chapter 25

"Chloe, you traitor! Where are you?" Valeska screams, "Show yourself!" As I enter the dining hall, I can see Valeska standing with her back turned toward me. Chloe is nowhere to be seen.

"Valeska!" I shout, sounding braver than I feel. I stand glaring at her as she turns to face me. My heart is pounding and my palms sweating. Behind Valeska, I see Chloe step into the room. She looks tired, like she's losing strength.

"I never thought you would betray me, Chloe," Valeska says, glancing back at her. She's holding Genevieve's crowbar in one hand and Sybil's knife in the other. Red and black blood is smeared on her face, arms, and clothes. Both weapons are dripping with it.

"I must say," she continues, "I'm very disappointed. We've been together since the beginning. Why now? Why throw everything away for her?"

"You crossed a line, Valeska," Chloe growls, "I'm only doing what I promised Maris I would do. Sybil can't help her, so it falls to me."

"There is no Maris anymore!" Valeska thunders, "Why do you care about her? You were a surgeon in life! You should have been granted access to the Oasis when you died! You risked your life to save others! She denied you what you deserved!"

"So now you care?" Chloe snarls, "After everything you said earlier? How humans are nothing but souls to reap? I know exactly why I was sent to the Plains. I was both a soldier and a surgeon. When I wasn't preserving life, I was taking it. I shot my enemies dead...even if they were incapacitated. That's why I was picked to protect you, Valeska. The same as any other Sentinel. Maris wanted loyalty with no hesitation to kill when necessary. And I'm prepared to kill you."

"Killing humans is easy," Valeska laughs, "Maybe you were good at that, but I'm more than just some measly human, Chloe!"

"You're just as mortal as one..." Chloe growls, "And here your powers are nullified. Maybe you can take more hits than an average woman, but that doesn't mean you can't be worn down. Even you have your limits!"

"Sybil couldn't stop me, and neither can you," Valeska taunts.

"You infected her like the parasite you are!" Chloe shrieks. She fires and the round grazes Valeska's cheek, embedding in the wall near me.

"Chloe...I'm going to give you one more chance," Valeska warns, "Lower your weapon or I swear I'll send you straight to the Abyss!"

"That's not going to happen," Chloe growls.

"Chloe, don't make me do this..."

"You have my answer!" Chloe snaps. Valeska sighs and hurls her knife straight at Chloe. The blade pierces her heart and she falls to her knees. She wraps her fingers around the handle and grits her teeth as she takes aim at Valeska. The revolver falls from her hand and clatters on the floor.

"Chloe..." I gasp. She pulls the knife loose and struggles to stand. One foot, then two. She teeters and looks up at Valeska.

"My, my...how noble..." Valeska drawls, "Don't kid yourself...you're not going to last much longer..."

"Shut up!" Chloe snarls. She hurls the knife at Valeska who catches it without so much as flinching. She casts it aside and it tumbles under a nearby table. Chloe falls to one knee and reaches for her revolver. Valeska calmly walks forward and kicks it away.

"I've seen enough..." she mutters, looking down at Chloe, "I have no patience for servants who disobey me. Once I'm finished here...I'll come find you in the Abyss..." She smashes the crowbar into the side of Chloe's head, splattering the floor and a nearby table with blood. A sickening crack echoes through the hall. She falls onto her side and both her body and revolver, begin to disintegrate.

"It's just you and me now, Wendy," Valeska says, turning to face me.

"You're not going to win..."

"Oh? Why is that?" Valeska taunts.

"Day and night, you'll never leave my sight," I recite, "By your side I will stand and fight. You'll never stay lost, wherever you roam, no matter the cost, I will bring you home. For I am your guardian, your teacher, your loyal friend. I will be there until the end." Valeska tucks the crowbar under her arm and gives a few slow, sarcastic claps.

"Very good, Wendy," she mocks, "The Oath of the Sentinels."

"The same one Sybil took when I was born," I continue, "The same one Chloe took when she met you."

"Your point?" Valeska snorts, taking the crowbar from under her arm. She and I lock eyes and begin circling.

"Sentinels dedicate themselves to us, Valeska," I growl, "That oath binds them to us for eternity; and they'll make any sacrifice to keep it."

"I hope you're going somewhere with this," Valeska sighs.

"When one of us comes of age, the Sentinel shifts from protector to adviser. A partner with whom we lead together," I continue, the two of us cease circling and stand facing one another, "I owe Sybil my life. Now that she's in danger, it's my turn to protect her."

"I suppose even I can respect that," Valeska admits, "but I wouldn't hold my breath if I were you. Besides...are you certain you want to rescue a murderer?"

"Sybil isn't a murderer!" I hiss.

"And again, you don't remember," Valeska mutters, shaking her head, "I truly wish I could just snap my fingers and give back everything you lost. It must be nice, being so blissfully ignorant of the past. I can honestly say I envy that. Tell me something, Wendy...have you ever wondered how a seventeen-year-old girl could be so proficient in the use of a knife?"

"She's been dead for years," I argue, "She's had plenty of time to practice."

"You're right...she's been dead for quite a while; but have you ever wondered how she got to the Plains? She must have done something wrong, don't you agree? You heard Chloe...she stained her hands with blood and look where she ended up. Sybil is no different. She committed five separate murders, each requiring a high level of skill with a knife."

"You're lying!" I snarl.

"Allow me to spell it out for you since you still can't remember," Valeska sneers, "Every Sentinel has a bloody history. Reika has blood on her hands too and you know it. She told you shortly before we met in the Abyss. I know because I was watching. Remember?" She's right...I do remember.

"So what?" I growl, "Maybe Reika is, but that doesn't prove that what you're saying about Sybil is true."

"I would tell you to ask her yourself, but I'm afraid that's out of the question," Valeska cackles, "Besides...I'm through talking..." Valeska charges at me with her crowbar raised over her head. I dodge the swing and she smashes apart a table. Another vicious swing damages a wall. I can't get a shot off, she's too close. I dodge a third swing and leap over one of the tables. She smashes it apart and I shoot her twice in the stomach. She howls and lunges for me. I trip her and she tumbles to the ground. The crowbar hooks around my ankle and she yanks my foot out from under me. I stumble backward and fire a single shot through her heart. She screams and scrambles to her feet. What is it going to take to stop her? I fire two more rounds into her chest and place the last one in her shin. She goes down on one knee and I flee the dining hall.

I make it to my room and slam the door behind me. Before Valeska can reach me, I've shoved the bed in front of the door. I can hear her pounding on the door while I struggle to reload my weapon. That's when I catch a glimpse of myself in the mirror. I'm older again, just like the dreams. With my revolver reloaded, I scramble to find the kitchen knife I keep in one of the desk drawers. Once I find it, I place it in my boot and fling open the window. As I'm crawling out, Valeska smashes a hole in the door. She tears another piece loose and I jump out onto the grass.

Moments later, Valeska bursts through the door and races for the window. I fire once and strike her in the chest, but it does little to slow her down. It's like I'm not making a difference. She just won't die. I turn and run alongside the building as she leaps out of the window. The ground begins to quake and both of us collapse. As I drag myself to my feet, a massive fissure opens up in the ground between us. The orphanage splits in two and begins to collapse. Rubble and debris rain down along the edge of the building as another nearby fissure opens up.

"It won't be long now!" Valeska cackles, "Go ahead! Run all you want!" She rushes forward and leaps over the fissure. She charges toward me and I dodge two vicious swipes before sprinting away from the building. A section of the orphanage crashes down where she and I once stood. The pouring rain soaks me to the bone and at least twice I slip on the grass and moss covered pavement. I duck into a small building and slam the door behind me. I glance out the window to see Valeska walking toward me.

"Is this what a true leader does?" Valeska taunts, stopping in the street, "Run away from a fight? The Plains deserves better than a coward!"

"You call me a coward?" I shout through the shattered window, "You're hiding in Sybil's body!" Valeska lets out a cackle.

"I only need her to regain my strength," Valeska explains, "Until then, your friend is under my control." She raises the crowbar and smashes the knob off the door. It swings open and Valeska lunges at me. The crowbar grazes my cheek. Another swing narrowly misses my neck as I hit my back against a wall.

Valeska swings and embeds the crowbar in the wall. I raise my weapon and shoot her twice. She shouts in pain and blood pours from the wounds. I grab her by the collar of her shirt and headbutt her in the nose. She drops the crowbar and wrestles for my gun. I bite her hand and punch her in the cheek. She hurls me into a wall and the gun falls to the floor. I kick the revolver toward the door and race to retrieve it. Valeska tackles me and we both reach for the weapon. I swat her hand away and snatch up the gun. She smashes my face into the pavement and I press the muzzle against her cheek. The blast leaves me unable to hear in one ear. She screams and I kick her off. She grabs my ankle and I fall to the ground. Her face has been ripped open by the blast. Blood is pouring from her mouth and both cheeks have gaping holes.

I roll onto my back and fire again. The round sails through her shoulder and she lets go. I kick her in the face and stumble to my feet before sprinting down the street. I'm down to my last few rounds. Valeska runs after me and I struggle to reload. Valeska chases me onto an adjacent street. Just up ahead, I can see that the street has collapsed into a massive sinkhole. I pound on the door to a nearby house and race to another when it refuses to open. Valeska leaps onto my back and we both crash to the pavement. My revolver falls from my hand and into the sinkhole. I elbow Valeska in the jaw and wrestle her off of me. I remove my knife from my boot and race to the nearest house. The door is ajar and I burst through it. I'm no longer in Cinder Valley. I'm standing in front of my old house. The sky is filled with clouds and the sun is only just visible behind them.

With Valeska right behind me, I sprint into the house and slam the door behind me. Holding the knife ready, I back away from the door as Valeska breaks it down. I charge at her with the knife, but I never hit my mark. She grabs my wrist and twists the knife from my hand. I try to pick it up before her, but she throws me to the floor. Flames begin to spread from the basement door. Smoke fills the room and the flames engulf the living room. Valeska laughs and waves the knife in a taunting manner. She charges and I manage to grab hold of her arm, but it's not enough to prevent the blade from slashing my forehead. Blood drips into my eye as I struggle to disarm her. I manage to throw her off and run to the front door. Before I can reach it, she grabs my arm and throws me against a wall. The two of us wrestle for control of the knife.

I slam my forehead into her nose and knock her to the floor. I sprint through the kitchen, overturning chairs and anything else I can find to slow her down. The smoke is becoming too thick to see. I try to open the back door and find that the lock is jammed. I throw my shoulder against it, but it does me no good. Valeska enters the kitchen. I pick one of the chairs up and slam it into her. She stumbles and I bring it down on her head. Through my fits of coughing, I throw the chair through the window and crawl out onto the back deck. Still gasping for air, I get to my feet and tumble down the stairs, landing in a heap on the grass. The back door crashes open and I look up to see Valeska. As I get to my feet, I see that my house isn't on the street I remember. It's perched on a pillar of rock high in the air. Valeska calmly walks down the flaming stairs, smirking the entire time.

"You ready to give up yet?" she laughs as she makes her way toward me. I back toward the edge of the cliff and glance down at the dense fog below.

"Long way to the bottom..." Valeska taunts, "Better watch your step!" She runs toward me and I brace myself. I try to step out of the way, but she predicts it. I'm left breathless as the knife pierces my stomach. I stumble backward and catch Valeska by the arm, pulling her over the edge of the cliff with me.

The two of us fall for several seconds and land in a large body of water. I sputter and gasp as I struggle to keep my head above the surface. The fog is so dense that it's impossible to tell if the shore is nearby. Before Valeska can take it back, I rip out the knife. The salt water stings as it seeps into my wounds. Valeska surfaces nearby and begins swimming toward me. I try to flee, but the pain in my stomach is blinding. She punches me in the nose and grabs my throat.

I take hold of her arms and try to pry her off. After a brief struggle, I manage to remove one of her hands, but only for a moment. Valeska forces my head below the surface. I spear her with the blade and she loosens her grasp. As I resurface, I gasp for air and slash her across the cheek. I loop my arm around her neck and jam the blade into her neck. She thrashes about, snarling and shouting. She sinks below the surface and I put the knife in my boot. The fog is beginning to clear and I can see a nearby dock. I start swimming toward it, terrified that Valeska might pull me under at any moment.

Once I reach the dock, I pull myself up and collapse. I'm so exhausted I can barely move. Even so, I know I have to get up. Hail begins to fall, and within seconds it begins to intensify. The sound of thunder echoes through the air. It takes everything I have to stand up, and when I do my heart skips a beat. Valeska surfaces nearby and pulls herself up onto the dock. She's bleeding profusely and clenching her fists. I draw my knife and hold it ready.

"I'm not through with you yet," she hisses, taking a step toward me, "I will not lose to you! I won't stop until you die!"

"Am I really that much of a threat to you?" I shout.

"Anyone who sides with Maris is a threat to all of existence!" Valeska shrieks, "You, Lydia, and Carmen! All of you! I'm sick of the way you all defend Maris! How you have such blind faith in humanity!"

"I don't know what you went through, but you're wrong!" I shout, "There are evil people in this world, Valeska! And you're one of them! But you're too blind to see it!" In that instant, a lightning bolt crashes down between us. The dock splinters and we're hurled away from the blast. When I get to my feet, the area around me has once again changed. I'm in the park, just down the street from Red Oak. Rain is still falling with an intense ferocity and lightning strikes are crashing down around the city. My knife is lying several feet away, the blade stuck in the grass. I scramble to my feet and pull it from the dirt. Valeska is nearby, staggering to her feet. Her breathing sounds labored and she's struggling to keep her balance. The earth quakes beneath us and we both stumble. She gives a smirk and begins walking toward me. I start backing away, keeping the knife ready in front of me.

"You've grown, Wendy..." Valeska growls, "If only I'd killed you back then. It would have been so much easier. If Maris hadn't caught on, I wouldn't have left so soon. I would have stayed and watched you die!" A lightning bolt strikes nearby, bits of dirt and grass rain down behind me. The flash blinds me and Valeska takes advantage of the distraction. She knocks me to the ground and tries to steal the knife from me. She rips it from my grasp and stabs me in the chest. I scream in pain and punch her in the jaw.

She yanks the knife out and stabs me again. This time I get a firm hold on her wrist and sink my teeth into it. She snarls and forces the blade further into my chest. She struggles to wrench the blade out and only worsens my wound. Within seconds I'm beginning to cough up blood. Valeska pulls the blade loose and tries to stab me again. This time I manage to stop her, but I'm losing strength. The blade inches closer and closer to my throat. With all my strength, I roll and push her off. The knife pierces my shoulder and I wrap my hands around her throat. I smash her head into the ground over and over again. She lets go of the knife and I snatch it up.

"You took everything from me!" I scream, pinning her to the ground, "You ruined my life! Annie is dead and my life fell apart around me! It's all your fault!" I stab the knife through her eye and she lets out one final scream. Her body goes limp and I pull the knife free. I collapse onto the ground beside her and stare up at the sky. I feel something on my leg and sit up to see Valeska's tar-black blood, now in the shape of a small snake, slithering away from Sybil's body. I drag myself to my feet, stumbling and trying to stay focused. My vision is getting blurry.

With the last of my strength, I charge forward and sink the knife into the blood. It squirms in pain and begins to crumbles as it turns to ash. The wind carries it away and I fall onto my side. I stare up at the sky through fits of coughing. My vision fades in and out. Just before losing consciousness, I can see a figure standing over me...

Chapter 26

"Wendy...wake up..." I groan and take a deep breath.

"Wendy...I know you can hear me..." I don't recognize the voice. I open my eyes and blink a few times. My vision comes into focus and I see a woman with long dark hair, brown skin, and green eyes kneeling beside me. She bears a slight resemblance to Valeska.

"Who are you?" I mumble. She helps me sit up and props me against a nearby tree.

"My name is Carmen," she answers, "I watch over the Oasis."

"Is...is this real?" I ask. Looking around, I see that I'm in the cemetery near Red Oak.

"You're still asleep," Carmen replies, "I suspect you won't be for much longer." I look down at my hands and examine my stomach. I still have blood on my arms and clothes, but my wounds have healed.

"So...you healed me?" I ask. Carmen nods.

"That I did," Carmen smiles.

"What happened to Maris? Is she okay? And the others! Sybil, Genevieve, Chloe...please tell me they're okay."

"They're just fine," Carmen assures me, "Lydia has already freed Maris, and she and Reika rounded up your friends. They're all safe."

"What about Annie?"

"You'll see her again soon," Carmen smiles, "but first...there's someone who wants to talk to you." I hear footsteps behind the tree and Sybil steps out where I can see her. She kneels down beside me and hugs me tight.

"I'm so happy you're okay," she quavers, "I couldn't do anything to fight her, I'm so sorry, Wendy!"

"It's okay..." I whisper, "I'm fine." She lets go and looks me in the eye.

"No!" Sybil sobs, "It's not okay! I screwed up! I failed you! I didn't do my job! You almost died because of me!"

"It was my fault, Sybil," I reply, "I went against my better judgment. I let Valeska escape."

"I should have done more," Sybil cries, "I'll do better next time, I promise!" She wipes tears from her eyes and looks down at her knees, "I was excited to be your Sentinel. It was an honor. Is an honor...that Maris placed that trust in me. I took it as an opportunity to make up for what I did..."

"So then...what Valeska said was true?" I ask. She nods.

"It's a long story," she replies, "It's true that I worked in a factory, but that was toward the end. My parents never got along. They fought one another right up until the end. My father was an architect. He met my mother while on vacation in England; a few years before I was born. They came to America four months later and got married soon after that. I was born a year later. Their marriage fell apart. My father fell ill and died when I was seven. My mother took me back to England with her a few months later."

"Why didn't you tell me?"

"I did," Sybil insists, "Do you remember?"

"I'm afraid not..."

"I never adjusted to life in England," Sybil continues, "What few friends I had, I left behind here in Virginia. I ran away from home when I was nine. I don't know why I did it. Maybe I was just upset with my mother. Looking back on it now, I realize what a bad idea it was... running away like that. I guess I just didn't know what I wanted."

"What happened after you left home?" I ask.

"I stole what I needed to survive, I got mixed up in some things I shouldn't have," Sybil explains, "It was a rough time in my life. At ten, I was attacked in the street. My food was stolen, my shoes, my money... all of it. I felt powerless. I wanted to make sure I could defend myself if I ever got into trouble again. That's when I started training myself to use a knife. I stole this from a vendor in town." She removes her knife from the sheath on her hip and places it on the ground in front of me. I recognize it as the same one Valeska used to kill Chloe. A large dagger with a round handle made of bone.

"What happened after that?"

"When I was fourteen, I did something stupid," Sybil continues, "Something that started me down a dark path. I got mugged again and this time I killed both of them. I was so angry that I went far beyond what was necessary. It wasn't even self-defense at that point, it was murder. I went on the run and eventually I was caught. I got violent with the other prisoners, my behavior was erratic at best. They sent me off to an institution for treatment. The doctors put me on these pills and something changed."

"What do you mean?"

"I mean I wasn't the same person after that," Sybil explains, "I just...I wasn't in my right mind. I stole the remainder of the medication about a month in and escaped. I spent several months wandering around, getting into other, stronger drugs. I was a mess. I started to get desperate. Eventually I found myself in London. Things only got worse from there. The next year was a blur. I was hallucinating, I was paranoid, nothing was right. I thought I was just having these really vivid nightmares. I would wake up in various places around the city, never knowing how I got there. It wasn't until...until I..." She buries her face in her hands.

"What is it?" I ask, "Sybil..."

"I came to my senses just after the last murder," Sybil cries, "I had her heart in my hand, blood all over my clothes, my hands...my knife. I hid the heart and ran until I couldn't run anymore. Every night for weeks after that, I would see the mangled bodies of my victims. I'm thankful that I can't sleep anymore. I found myself at a hospital after I cleaned myself up. I went into withdrawal and received treatment for it. I stowed away on a ship to New York once I was well enough. I came back to Cinder Valley and that's when I got my job at the factory. I was only there for five months before the accident. After I died...this is where I was buried." She stands up and helps me to my feet. Carmen watches as Sybil leads me to a nearby headstone. Looking down at it, I see that it's hers:

Sybil Mabel Clarence
Born - January 9, 1873
Died - April 30, 1890

"I always felt like I deserved it," Sybil whispers, placing her hand on her neck wound, "Every day in the Plains felt like a blessing. I was so sure I belonged in the Abyss for what I did. So when Maris approached me, I was confused. Why would she want someone like me to watch over her own child?" Another tear rolls down her cheek. I wrap my arms around her and hug her tight.

"She knew you had a good heart, Sybil," I assure her, "And I'm glad I met you." I glance at Carmen for a moment and spot a tall Egyptian woman speaking with Carmen. She looks to be in her early forties, her hair is black, and she's wearing a dark cloak and heavy boots. On one hip is a short sword, on the other, a flintlock pistol. Judging from her clothing, she looks like she might have lived toward the end of the 1700's. I recognize her, but at first I can't remember her name. I let go of Sybil and she notices me staring at the woman.

"You don't remember her, do you?"

"She's familiar...but I can't remember her name," I reply, "All I know is she's Carmen's Sentinel."

"Her name is Malaika," Sybil smiles, "She's quiet, but every bit as warm as Carmen. She was a bounty hunter in life." Carmen and Malaika end their discussion and begin walking toward us.

"We should get going," Carmen says. She motions for us to follow. Looking back near the tree, I catch a glimpse of Annie's grave. The statue still seems so eerie, even in the sunlight.

"Come on, Wendy," Carmen beckons, "There's more for you to see."

Chapter 27

"What do you remember so far?" Carmen asks me as we exit the cemetery.

"Not everything, I can say that much," I admit, "I know how I got here, I remember the fires, the hospital...but I don't understand why I was trying to come back to Cinder Valley." I close the gate behind me and follow after them.

"Anything else?" Carmen asks.

"The train crashed and I fell into a coma," I answer, "Annie died and...I...I couldn't save her. I was right there and there was nothing I could do."

"You didn't stand there and watch, you tried to save her," Sybil says, "Even though it meant scarring yourself forever, you tried with all your might to save your friend...and Annie knows that."

"Keep going, Wendy," Carmen says, "Tell us what else you remember."

"I know Sybil saved me the night my aunt and uncle died," I continue, "I still can't remember the entire argument, but I know I must have had a poor reaction when Sybil first told me of her past. That was shortly before I got on the train. I remember surviving the fire at Red Oak, and what Valeska did to me. I remember finding a new home after I left the hospital, but I don't remember much about it."

"One of the nurses and her husband ended up adopting you," Sybil explains, "They both took care of you after the fire at Red Oak. Your recovery was miraculous to them. You lived with them until you were twenty. After that, you left to live on your own."

"Something tells me things didn't go very well," I murmur.

"You started drinking," Sybil continues, "You stopped coming to the Plains and I started to get worried. Annie's death took a heavy toll on you. At twenty-three, you boarded a train and decided to come back to Cinder Valley...for good..."

"After Chloe found me, I had a dream...maybe it was more of a vision, I'm not sure," I say, "In it I was standing in Red Oak with you, Sybil. We were talking, but I couldn't hear what was being said. All I know is that it was after I left the hospital. That was where I saw myself next. Lying in a hospital bed. But what had me baffled was what came after that. I found myself on the train again, and this time there were two numbers. A twenty-three written in blood, and a twenty-five written in black ink. I suppose I understand the twenty-three now...but what about the twenty-five?"

"Twenty-five is the age you're to take over rule of the Ashen Plains," Sybil explains, "That must be what it meant." We come to a halt and I look up at the ruins of Red Oak. Many of the windows are cracked and broken. The bricks are covered with moss and grime and various parts of the structure are scorched from the fire.

"This way, Wendy," Carmen beckons. I take a deep breath and follow everyone up the front steps. Carmen pushes open the door and Sybil and I walk inside with Malaika just behind us. Standing in the dining hall, is Lydia, Maris, and everyone else. Chloe waves to me and Eliza runs up and hugs me.

"I'm so happy you're okay!" Eliza squeals. Franklin and Tom both come to greet me. Claire, Brian, and Genevieve stand up from one of the tables and come to join us. Grenda and Glenda are standing against a far wall. They both wave to me. Glenda's arms are all healed up and the needles have been removed. Everyone is here...all except one...

"Where's Annie?" I ask.

"She's upstairs," Genevieve answers.

"Yeah, she's waiting for you on the roof," Tom adds. Claire gives me a light shove toward the stairs.

"Go on," Claire smiles, "Don't keep her waiting." I head toward the stairs and to the roof. It takes me a minute to find the door. Once I do, I place my hand on the handle and take a deep breath. I pull open the door and head up the stairs. Sunlight is flowing in through a crack in the exit. I push it open and the sunlight blinds me. My eyes adjust as I step onto the roof and I see Annie standing near the edge. She turns to face me, her lips curling into a smile as I run up and hug her.

"It's good to see you," she smiles. Her smile fades and she averts her gaze.

"So...it wasn't just a dream?" I ask. I already know the answer, but I still just wish she would tell me it was.

"I'm sorry, Wendy..." she murmurs, "It was bad enough the first time...but now it must be like it happened all over again."

"I'm the one who should be sorry. If I'd found you sooner...then maybe...maybe things would be different."

"You can't spend your life replaying that night over and over again in your head," Annie says, placing a hand on my shoulder, "It'll just tear you up again. When I found out what happened to you, I felt terrible. I knew my death had an impact, but I never realized how strong. I just hope you can forgive me...and not just me, but everyone else."

"Why would I need to forgive you or anyone else?" I ask, "I understand now. It's been rough. I was remembering bits and pieces over the past two days and...well...it was difficult. I can't imagine being told everything all at once. You did the right thing. You all did."

"It wasn't supposed to happen so fast," Annie explains, "We intended for things to play out much longer. For two months, there was almost nothing. You just kept having that dream about the train. I'll admit, we were starting to get worried...but we never expected that Linda or Valeska would interfere."

"Well, what was the plan?" I ask, "How did it all come together?" Annie takes a deep breath and exhales.

"After you fell into a coma, you came to see Sybil in the Plains," Annie explains, "You had reverted back to your sixteen-year-old self. You couldn't find me and asked where I was. That's when we realized you had lost part of your memory. Sybil spoke with Maris about it and she decided to go along with what happened; recreate that time in your life. Carmen released me from the Oasis and allowed me to come visit, so as to maintain the illusion that you were still sixteen. Your body was mangled and we feared that the shock of regaining your memories all at once could kill you. So we felt it best to let you remember on your own. Everyone was told what happened. Claire, Tom, Franklin, Sybil, Genevieve, Brian, and Eliza. They were all given instructions on what to do. Maris said that you were still somehow linked to the Ashen Plains, and that there was a risk that Shadows could invade your mind and cause irreparable harm."

"I...was still connected?" I ask, "How is that possible?"

"Maris explained it to me after you fell into your coma," Annie explains, "She suspected that you may have tried to open a portal to the

Plains after you heard the explosion on the train. It didn't open all the way and somehow things got mixed up after you lost consciousness. As time went on, some of Linda's followers invaded your mind, and Sybil drove them off."

"The library," I whisper, "So I was right. She was looking for Shadows." Annie nods.

"We all came together to keep you safe," Annie continues, "Someone always remained behind to guard the entrance to your mind. That's why Claire visited so often. Sybil had to stay close to you, so Claire and Franklin would often take shifts protecting your mind from intruders. Once you began to notice the presence of Shadows in your memory of Red Oak, we knew you were making progress. I was a little surprised by Claire's sudden decision to track down Glenda, but I know she didn't think it would cause as much damage as it did. We couldn't just tell you what was going on. Sybil and the others did such a great job of protecting you that it infuriated Linda. So she threw us into the Abyss. After that, the rest is history."

I glance at the edge of the building and walk toward it. I look down at the courtyard and Annie grabs my arm. I turn to face her and see that she has tears forming in her eyes. I take one last look at the courtyard and step away from the ledge.

"Please don't..." she breathes.

"Sybil said that I was coming back here 'for good'," I murmur, "I know what she meant now. When I got on that train, I had a plan. I was going to come back home and visit this place one last time. I was coming back to end it..." Annie pulls me further away from the ledge and clings to my arm.

"You probably knew this when you got on the train," she says, "but... if you did die now, you would likely go to the Oasis. You wanted to see me again, didn't you?" I nod and feel my eyes begin to well up with tears.

"It was stupid," I admit, "but that's what I thought..." Annie loosens her grasp and looks me in the eye.

"Well now's your chance to decide," Annie replies, "You can jump off the roof and give up, or you can continue forward and head downstairs. Leap from the roof and you'll never wake from your coma. You'll pass away in your sleep. I know that's not you, though. You've never been one to give up. You always persevere. I can't be sure that we'll ever see each other again, but I want you to promise me something."

"What?"

"Promise me that you'll get a new start on life," she replies, "Promise me that you will find a way to keep going. Don't let what happened to me ruin you. You're better than that, Wendy. You have so many others who are here for you. Sybil, Genevieve, Tom, Claire, Franklin, they'll always be there for you. Don't put so much focus on me. I know it's hard, but you have to let me go. I'll miss you too, but I don't want to go back to the Oasis and wonder if you ever pulled yourself out of this rut. Can you do that?"

"I promise..." I whisper. She hugs me and leads me back down to the dining hall. At this point, everyone but Maris, Lydia, and Carmen have vanished.

"Where is everyone?" I ask as Annie and I enter the hall.

"They're around," Maris smiles as she approaches us, "You'll see them again soon enough. Have you two finished with your goodbyes?" We both nod and Maris places her hand on my head.

"Good," she whispers, "It's time to wake up, Wendy..." I close my eyes and suddenly my body feels heavy. My leg and ribs are aching. My eyes flutter open and I'm lying in a hospital bed. I stare up at the ceiling and slowly turn my head to the left. Sybil is sitting in a chair beside my bed.

"So...what now?" I croak. She and I exchange grins, and that's when I notice Maris standing at the foot of my bed.

"Rise and shine, Wendy," she smiles, "You've got a long recovery ahead of you. Better rest up while you can..."

Epilogue

Two weeks have passed since I awoke from my coma. My injuries finished healing at a rapid pace; so quickly that the medical staff saw it as miraculous. This earned me a great deal of attention that I didn't care for. Doctors started examining me, trying to figure out the reason for my rapid recovery. Eventually the day that I was to be released arrived, but things didn't go the way I'd hoped. For the first two days after awakening, things seemed just fine. Not long after that, the full weight of what had occurred came crashing down upon me. I was plagued with nightmares, flashbacks, panic attacks, the sort of things I had tried so hard to cover up through drinking. I was beginning to realize why it was that I'd considered suicide the day I boarded that train.

Pieces of my memory are still returning. Things I'd forgotten about, things I don't want to remember. Valeska was right...I do have blood on my hands. I was nothing short of a monster. Before I lost my memory, I had no regard for those around me. The fire at Red Oak, Annie's murder, it changed me into someone I didn't recognize. I was walking a path eerily similar to Valeska. Just the thought is enough to make me shudder. After Sybil told me who I was, who my mother was, I wasn't sure what to say. I called Sybil every name in the book, told her that she was a traitor for keeping my history a secret, said I never wanted to see her again...and that was the end of it. I thought she left, but it turns out she followed me onto the train that day. She went with me to the hospital, stayed nearby the entire time.

My internal struggles soon caught the attention of the medical staff. It started with me waking up screaming one night. From that point on, they watched me like hawks, took notes on my condition, the works. The day I was to leave, I was escorted to the front of the building where two men were waiting for me. One of them was Dr. Fulmer, the shrink Red Oak had sent me to so long ago. The years hadn't been kind to him, but there was no mistaking those cold blue eyes, nor that vile smirk he always wore. We had ourselves a brief exchange, said he just wanted to talk to me. I knew better. I was led into a nearby room with one of the hospital doctors, Fulmer himself, and the man I assumed to be an associate of his.

After Fulmer finished asking me a series of questions, he beckoned for his associate to step closer, whispered something in his ear, and the next thing I knew, I was being grabbed by both arms and led out to the front of the building. I spit in Fulmer's face and told him he'd regret his decision to commit me. Still weak from my time in the coma, there was little I could do. I landed a few heavy blows to Fulmer before I was finally restrained. Curses were shouted, chairs were upended, and blood was spilled. I was dragged outside and forced into the back of a waiting truck. I fought to get free with every ounce of my strength, but there was nothing I could do. As my captors were attempting to force the doors closed, I noticed Sybil standing several feet behind them. Her arms crossed and her gaze focused on the ground in front of her.

"Sybil!" I shrieked, "Sybil, what the hell are you doing? Sybil!" Just before the doors closed, she glanced up at me with a look of sorrow. I couldn't hear over the shouts of my captors, but it didn't matter. I could read her lips just fine.

"I'm sorry, Wendy," she said. The doors closed and soon the vehicle began to move. I was on my way to Brookfield Asylum...